THE GRAMMAR OF FAITH

THE
GRAMMAR
OF
FAITH

Paul L. Holmer

1817

Published in San Francisco by

HARPER & ROW, PUBLISHERS

New York, Hagerstown, San Francisco, London

FIRST EDITION

Designed by Jim Mennick

Library of Congress Cataloging in Publication Data

Holmer, Paul L.
   THE GRAMMAR OF FAITH.

   1. Theology—Addresses, essays, lectures. I. Title.
BR85.H574   230   78-3351
ISBN 0-06-064003-0

78 79 80 81 82 10 9 8 7 6 5 4 3 2 1

To
Paul, Linnea, and Jonathan

Contents

Preface

The word *grammar* in the title of this book might seem puzzling. I use the word because Graham Wallas (1858–1932), a professor of political science in London, accustomed one of my early teachers to the notion that there was a "grammar of politics," a kind of schematic sense, despite irrational social forces and irresponsible attitudes. Karl Pearson's *Grammar of Science* (1892) was one of the first philosophic books I bought. Though I read it too young to understand all of it, I was made aware of patterns of thinking and discovery that were unexpected and even thrilling. Then John Henry Newman's *Grammar of Assent* (1870) proposed that "assenting," of all things, was deeply ruled, despite the random appearances to the contrary. With diverse reading, it was not hard to get used to an extended use of the term *grammar!*

But Ludwig Wittgenstein's careful use of *grammar* in the *Philosophical Investigations* gave a new impetus and a more careful set of considerations to go with the expression. A leading thought of his book suggests that quite primitive instances of the language of faith and the life of faithful believers answer to one another. Both belong to a single grammar. But to comment upon that fittingness—the "how" and "what"—is also a good part of second-level theology, dogmatic and formal though it might appear. This academic and teaching kind of theology, important in its place, is properly parasitic upon the Bible and upon other instances where the use of language is part of the faith and not just about it. But it states the grammar of religious living and thinking.

These pages would not have been written if certain kinds of academic theology were not such a scandal. Two features of what passes for theology in the modern world have long bothered me. One is the radical disagreement among theologians. There are competing "isms," contradictions, meta-views—generally an intellectual jumble. All of that reminds me of the kind of teaching I assimilated in philosophy, where reigning systems were thought to be irreducible and options were loosely paraded in the textbook culture we all imbibed and even taught. Much of the fecundity in theology also looks like speculation, some like senseless system-mongering, an awful lot like talking without even doing the hard job of ascertaining the relevant criteria. Some of this goes on still largely unchecked.

The other feature is that much of the academic theology has been discussed as if it had to do with the fundamentals of faith, hence its lofty pretense and hold upon the imagination of students and the hapless laity. It all purports to have to do with God and eternity; yet it soon produces a deep and pervasive religious skepticism. Or one has to become a teacher and make a virtue out of the disagreement. This reminds me again of much of the plausible philosophy I once learned and, unfortunately, also taught. Such a characteristic of schemes of thought suggests profound logical flaws. But, in theological arenas, such loosely articulated schemes of ideas become a slander upon the actual life of Christian belief and morals; and also, upon the plain fact that certainty, not doubt, ought to obtain when one knows God. The fundamentals of faith are misstated in such contexts of learning. Old-fashioned but perennial questions of "truth," "objectivity," "knowing God," etc., have been skirted and even shirked in this mad cacophony of voices. I hope that these pages will bring back such issues in a new and viable form.

It is downright silly to have Kierkegaard, Augustine, Wittgenstein, even analytic philosophy and contemporary logic, all used to please dilettantes, to justify relativism, and to make arbitrary choosing the name of the game. So these pages go after another morphology of the life of Christian belief, a logic and a grammar that we miss often because a monstrous illusion is fostered by a pattern of thought and speech, wherein objectivity, fact, meaning, truth, and even faith are advertised but never delivered. I can only hope that the thinkers noted, plus something of contemporary thought and logic, will, even if technical and difficult, make a tougher grammar of faith more apparent here, and even plausible. Obviously that supposes careful reflection by the reader, and what understanding comes will certainly have to belong to him or her. It would be odd, however, if that understanding were not partially coextensive with what any of us could also realize if we were plainly honest about ourselves and also sought God with all our heart, soul, mind, and strength. In religious matters, as well as some moral concerns, the criteria—even the light on very important concerns—are laid down somewhat differently. Unless we are prepared for that our theological reflection skitters off. We are misled by analogies again.

These essays are polemical. Some might complain that nothing constructive is being proposed. True, there is no ideology here; but what is said ought to fit much of Catholic, Lutheran, Calvinist, and evangelical convictional reflection. Aspects of Old Testament belief and life are not totally outside of my concern either. The logical difficulties, as I see them, are ecumenical and are a part of the landscape, even the ecology, of much learned talk about Christianity (and Judaism) today. I am deciding here neither all theological issues nor the internecine controversies, but I would like to give them a better setting. I am also anxious to get the themes of the Bible and the early creeds of Christendom lively once more. Such an ecumenical faith as believing in God and in Jesus Christ (not only in doctrines about God or in Christologies), is what the pseudo-learning of our day (historical, Biblical, theological, even logical) has made implausible. The concepts of "believe" and "know," "foundations" and "God," all have blurred for us. The aim, then, is constructive indeed, albeit indirect and rather modest.

Essays one, two, seven, and nine have not been published. They were read as lectures at Oxford University and under other titles at philosophical and theological meetings in Chicago, San Francisco, New York City, and the University of California (Santa Barbara). Students at Yale University, the University of Copenhagen, and the universities of Minnesota, Wisconsin, Chicago, and Michigan were discussants for much of the rest too. Earlier versions of several of the chapters have been published elsewhere: "Theology and Belief" as "Language and Belief" in *Theology Today*, Vol. 22 (October 1965), reprinted by permission of *Theology Today*, and in *Essays on Kierkegaard*, edited by Jerry H. Gill (Minneapolis: Burgess Publishing Co., 1969); "Scientific Language and the Language of Religion" in *Journal for the Scientific Study of Religion*, Vol. 1 (October 1961); "Metaphysics and Theology" in *Lutheran Quarterly*, Vol. 17 (1965); "Language and Theology" in *Harvard Theological Review*, Vol. 58 (1965); and "Theology, Atheism, and Theism" as "Atheism and Theism" in *Lutheran World*, Vol. 13 (1966).

My subsequent books, under the titles of *Logic and the Theologians* and *Philosophy and the Theologians* will augment the themes struck here.

It would be most surprising if my debt to colleagues and teachers, students and authors, was not apparent. But a remark of Scipio's, the statesman and conqueror of Hannibal at Zama (202 B.C.), is appropriate. He said that he was never less idle than when he had nothing to do, and never less lonely than when he was by himself. The reflections in these pages have mostly come about when attempts were being made to make sense for and by myself.

PAUL L. HOLMER

March, 1978

I

What Theology Is and Does

Many of us today, in the churches, universities, and seminaries, might share that unfortunately fetching point scored against theology when the young pastor-candidate suggests that psychology or sociology is more appropriate for him than theology because of his or her great love for people. For the popular view is that theology is painfully abstract, that it is a specialist's domain, that it is impractical, that it is of no use to the laity, and that it is about matters that do not and cannot concern those who are nonacademic. The upshot of this highly general view of theology is that it is juxtaposed against social action, against practice, against the plain loving of people, and against empirical studies. And then theology is (just as unfortunately) lumped with speculative concerns, with metaphysics, with subjectivity and special interests, and, by its detractors, finally, with astrology, prescientific thought, mythology, and make-believe.

More than this, theology at best does not quite seem like a discipline. Instead, it looks like free creation. Quite often, and especially recently, we have had theology identified with the revocation of familiar moral convictions, with God-is-dead views, and with the informal and almost shapeless meanderings of those who are making proposals for how the world ought to be. Suddenly, churches like the Roman Catholic, the Anglican, the Lutheran, and the European Reformed group have also begun to lose their control and authority in theological matters. In the name of theology, there is now a vast array of teachings, not quite in agreement with one another, but all of them bidding for attention within these groups. It is very hard, indeed, to make sense of it all. Theology looks almost promiscuous even where confessional views, Biblical allegiance, and Christian authority are loudly asserted. For even these time-honored safeguards and criteria have been caught up in the whirl of ideas that counts as theology.

But this matter can be put more baldly. There is something rather alarming also about the fact that theology, which is supposed to be foundational, is so loosely practiced in seminaries and colleges that one can tolerate diametrically opposed schools of thought. It certainly was one thing to have Lutherans, Calvinists, and Catholics contending; but at least there was a semblance of argument amid the acrimony. Besides, the positions were identifiable and the disagreements were often responsible and considerate. But now there is seldom either acrimony or argument. Much of what we thought was standard and minimal, a kind of point of departure, is no longer quite that. There is hardly anything but the sight of theologians talking past one another. Now, in the name of theology, we can espouse worldliness; by theologizing, we can aver that God is dead; via theology, we can declare that Scripture is mythology; and through erstwhile theological reflection, we can find symbols everywhere and little to be symbolized. The irony of all this is, indeed, that theology looks like free creation and is not so much true as it is obnoxiously interesting. And an air of tolerance settles over the entire array, almost as if it makes slight difference what is believed.

No wonder, then, that ministers often find theology to be something they can do without. For they take a risk in getting in on an "ism" that will be outmoded in another decade, or lost in a point of view that will be subsequently judged to be only an idiosyncrasy of a person or a school. Slight as the advantage may be, it is less taxing and often more reasonable just to settle for the protocols of church—baptism, confirmation, worship service, weddings, and funerals—and let them frame the Gospel and suggest their own future. By getting enough Bible to get by, some knowledge of people, and a generous dose of "knack," it looks suspiciously as if one can be a preacher *sans* all theology save the barest consciousness of whoever was one's churchly progenitor, be it Luther, Calvin, Wesley, Barth, or a nameless consensus.

The fact is that there is immense conceptual confusion in this area. Where everything counts as theology, we can safely say that scarcely anything really counts. Clearly, we have become uncertain of the criteria or even whether there are any at all. More than this, we have slipped into a whole nest of views, not strictly theological in themselves but *about* theology—views that are unexamined, widespread, and dubious. I refer here to such notions as the ambiguous one that we have theologies for every age and for every culture; or the strange view that theology is properly "yours" or "mine," somehow a personal or social expression; or the even more bizarre outlook that suggests that theology cannot help being fragmented and the way it is because the meaning of Christianity is so immense, so manifold, etc., that no one scheme of thought can do it justice.

Even more insidious and poorly conceived is the deeply skeptical and quasi-sophisticated view that develops in the most urbane university centers for the study of religions and their teachings. In such places, the sheer opulence of points of view and the thick harvest of historical antecedents give a revivification by scholarship and cause dim overviews to develop about the development of doctrine and the necessity that one succeed another. After a while, it becomes a lot easier to believe this vague metaview that makes one skeptical about any particular theology of an individual or a church than it is to be a lively believer and hearty participant in any one theology and its related practices. The point that seems so disturbing here is that these chaotic developmental views are so easy to teach and that they are no longer linked up with anything save the most obvious accommodation to the "Zeitgeist." They serve also to divorce most people from the practice of religion itself, and instead create a sophisticated clientele that is interested in theology as one more artifact cast up in the course of time.

This development is something like the phenomenon we see in

philosophy. Where once men philosophized in order to become
wise, now, after centuries of philosophizing, the quest for wisdom
gets lost in trying to keep the philosophies straight. Becoming wise
would be almost as surprising and as embarrassing—certainly as
unexpected—an outcome of the academic study of philosophy as
becoming a believer would be out of the academic study of
theology. No wonder, then, that the uses of theology have sometimes seemed a little remote to students and to churchmen. The
cause of this remoteness is not simply ignorance or stubbornness or
the refusal to learn. Instead, I wish to state with utmost finality
that the learned also have a responsibility here. The subject itself
has lost its substance; and its own logic has become blunted by
misuse and confused by the learned themselves.

Against and within such contexts, then, I wish to place these
remarks about what theology does and what, therefore, it is. These
notes could be said to be in the direction of defining theology
anew. It goes without saying, perhaps, that these notes also bear
heavily in the direction of providing the logic of theology. By this
logic, I hope to be saying again something about what theology is.

I I

There is a sense in which plainly and unequivocally theology is
interpretation. But we must be careful about that word *interpretation.* For I am not suggesting that everybody must interpret
always, or that all understanding involves interpretation, or even
that each person is entitled to his own interpretation. The word
interpretation is much used, and invariably to justify widely
divergent views, as when we say: "Each to his own interpretation." My remarks here are in another direction altogether.

I have noted that theology is interpretation. It is proper to ask:
"of what?" And there is a great deal to be said in response. There
is a kind of historical accounting that can be given of the history
of some Middle Eastern peoples, subsequently called Jews. Their
vicissitudes—slavery, wars, wanderings, exile, victories, and de-

feats—can be seen in a variety of contexts and can be adjudicated for a rich variety of purposes. For the moment, I do not wish to suggest that the historical scene, even of the ancient Jews, is plain and unequivocal. My point is that it is one kind of game in which the telling of the story is done only to fill out the account of Middle Eastern history, and quite another to tell it in order to make the reader a part of a community of faith, Jewish or Christian. In the former game, one addresses curiosity, one serves the interest of being accurate, and one provides an explanation of how people got the way they did, granted their time and circumstances. For the moment, let us call even this historical accounting an interpretation.

But when I tell the story, maybe the same story even down to the details, so that one will emulate the ancients' courage, live their virtues, eschew their vices, find their law, and seek their God with might and finesse of spirit, then I am doing something quite different. Another game is being played. This is, then, also an interpretation. When one presses on to the life of Jesus, to the fate of the Apostles, and to the teachings of Peter and Paul and their missionary lives, then, too, one can play a variety of games with the extant material.

It is important to note that nothing esoteric or rare is supposed here by the word *interpretation*. So, for example, it is not being supposed that "interpretation" is the only way to get "meaning," or that "interpreting" is a subtle intellectual necessity to get some kind of scheme going on otherwise neutral facts. Such pictures are falsifying. There are lots of things wrong about such suggestive pictures. For one thing, there are no neutral facts, bare, feature-less, utterly void of meaning, and utterly disengaged. As we shall note, the popular conviction is that science is about only the facts, whereas the humanities, morals, literature, and theology are interpretations and hence attempts to state the meanings. This is a dual conviction, unremittingly confused and false. In theological arenas it is widely believed that historical and critical studies get at the facts—and these again are said to be basic—whereas

theology states the meanings. The former are thought to be
objective and neutral; the latter, if not outright subjective, at least
a construct, probably intuitive, inventive, confessional, and surely
a party view. But here again the errors are egregious and difficult
to assess; for they involve subtle conceptual matters and strange
loyalties to the ethos and ground plan of our crafts and disciplines.
To attack this distinction is like fighting a supposition of a whole
age and of the modern universities.

For if there are neutral facts, discerned by a science, then it
would indeed look as if theology were an interpretation. Once
more, we can invoke a distinction—facts versus interpretation—
and assume that when I ask for facts, I do not want an interpretation. If I want an interpretation, it seems, I am asking for a
scheme within which the facts begin to bear upon something or
other, to mean something, and then they lose their neutrality.
Admittedly, this is a very tempting general intellective scheme,
within which we can fit a lot of detail. But I am declaring it to be
falsifying and misleading—even though it is almost unquestioned;
and it is given axiomatic importance in many places.

Interpretation is not the way we get meanings out of supposed
facts that otherwise have no meaning. Instead, there are a variety
of procedures, skills, questions, expectations, and attitudes that get
woven together into very general patterns. These we can learn
about. The broad names for two of these that concern us here are
"historical studies" (and I lump a lot of things therein) and
theology; but I could go on to specify a variety of other disciplines
and ways of understanding. The point is that both of these are like
games in one respect—namely, that therein we can play the field
according to the rules. But there is no subgame basic to all the rest.
There are, instead, interpretations: one way that is theological,
where everything is referred to God and the Godly life; another
way that is historical, where another set of concerns about
antecedents and consequences, causes and effects, and how "this"
became "that" are entertained. This latter game is a newer one,
for it has been realized only within the past couple of centuries in

an obvious public way. But today it is widely teachable and rather easily practiced by large numbers of historians and students. Both ways explain, expound, and make things clear. The point is that they do their tasks differently.

If modern scholarship is insistent upon any one thing these days, it is that we must think about everything of the past in an historical way. It is by virtue of a general "historical" outlook that most of us have come to think that we need the history of something or other before we can understand it. So we agree that we can never really know a writer or an episode or an event unless we know the time. We seem to be especially convinced in this way about writers, but, in an analogous way, about almost everything else in the past too. Only when we have done our utmost to think as an *age* thought and felt, do we feel entitled to assert what an author thought and felt. Only then can we even venture an estimate of the true significance of a writer's work. This is a great change in outlook, and it is certainly a good one if the alternative was that just anybody was free to extract whatever he thought appropriate from Sophocles, Shakespeare, the Psalmist, and the Apostle Paul.

But I wish to interject another note. In much of scholarship today, whether about ancient Jews, early Christians, Homer, or Alexander Pope, we tend to interpret the materials, or let us say, place them into a certain game, the historical-critical game or interpretation. I am not suggesting that it is trivial because it is a game; on the contrary, it is the mode and manner of most contemporaries with even a little education. It is done rather easily, though often badly, because we now have literature, techniques, trained teachers, and sufficient leisure, to do it. My only negative point is the slight one that this is surely not the necessary and sufficient way to understand everything and everybody. For the kind of understanding this yields is just that—a certain kind of understanding, and there are several kinds and ways of understanding. Because we can do this sort of thing for the Old Testament and the New does not mean we are closer to understanding them truly. Instead, it only means that we can now understand them historically.

Undoubtedly there are cases where we need information; and an unaided twentieth-century intelligence and a sympathetic imagination are not enough. But as in Shakespeare, so in the Bible, the passages where we would blunder badly if we were unequipped with a particular set of facts about the past seem to me to be rarer than is often thought, but undoubtedly they do exist. It is not true, however, that to understand the Scriptures historically is to get at the foundational matter. For historical study does yield a kind of understanding, but it is an historical understanding and usually nothing more. There is no such thing (if I can be bold and assertive) as "the" understanding. Just as there are no bare facts, subliminal and brutish, so there is no single understanding, plain and unrequited. There are, instead, historical facts and theological facts, and there are, indeed, an historical understanding of the Scriptures and a theological understanding of those same pages. And which is antecedent to which is an issue that cannot be settled on any large scale.

My point in brief is that obviously Christians have a large stake in theology. As will be indicated, theology does several things; but among them is the task of interpreting the Scriptures so that Paul, Jews, Greeks, Apostles, and the sundry writers and actors are put into the game they were playing. But they were in several games. They were participants in a Graeco-Roman culture, actors in a Near Eastern society, heirs to things Jewish, and apostles of the Lord Jesus. One can describe them, truthfully and tellingly, in their historical garb, and one can assess their words in a matrix that is historical. Most importantly, for Christian purposes, they were preachers and evangelists, apostles and Christians; and by virtue of convictions, passions, beliefs, and God-centeredness they also wrote and taught so that all might become like themselves—save, as the Apostle Paul said, these chains. Theology is that discipline in which the believers declare what the facts are, what the hopes, fears, and loves are, what the beliefs are, for those who find God in Christ Jesus. Believers are clearly in a life-and-death game of salvation.

Theology is, then, an interpretation. But not as if it were willful, episodic, or subjective. Theology is that skein of thought and language in which Christians understand themselves, the Bible, God, and their everyday world. Clearly, that kind of thought began for Christians with peculiar authority in the New Testament (with obvious debts to the older Scriptures, too). Historical and critical studies play quite a different game with the texts and the periods, one that surely can be played but is not the peculiar Christian game. For theology is that interpretation and that game which we all must play if we are to refer our lives to God.

Theology does not at every juncture demand an historical-critical understanding before it can be reasserted in our day. To make that case supposes far too standardized a view. As I have noted, there may be instances of literature, New Testament and Old, Shakespeare, Molière, or Plato, where one needs to know the time and occasion before one gets the drift of what was said. But these are particular instances where historical understanding is a necessary priority. Most instances of the New Testament, for example, are not like that. One suspects that it is far more important than most historical material to learn to hunger and thirst for righteousness, to learn to love a neighbor, and to achieve a high degree of self-concern, in order to understand the religious themes of the New Testament. There are, in short, personality qualifications that are also required. Perhaps it is even essential to have learned guilt because one has not done as he ought to have done. In any case, these forms of human consciousness are closer to the prerequisites for a Christian's understanding than is most knowledge supplied by other scholars.

Theology is interpretation, but only in the sense that it construes the Bible as though it were addressed to sinners, not the curious; to the ill who need a physician, not to those who are well and self-assured; to those who want to redeem their lives, not to the idlers who are looking for exciting ways to spend them. But this is not the whole story. Ears—not least of all, *modern* ears— are also deaf to the good tidings. So there are other things for the office of the theologian.

I I I

All of us have heard the modern lament over theology. The view is often bandied about that the failure of the churches to attract people is due to the fact that theology is outmoded, that it is unscientific and generally quaint. I agree that there is a strong case against theology if it is glaringly antique, prescientific, mythlike, and everything but modern. But this is a big supposition and has to be examined carefully indeed. Also, there have been a variety of views suggested by erstwhile theologians to meet this supposed condition. I call this condition "supposed" because I find it poorly defined, badly described, and, consequently, never addressed in any fundamental way by even those who are striving hardest to do so.

Especially does the diagnosis look ambiguous when you consider what people do in the name of modern theology. Sometimes we get theology redone around philosophers who are presently in favor. Or we get "process" theology to accord with "process" philosophy. Then we get empirical theologies when empiricism is "in" just as we once got highly logicized schemes in the Middle Ages when deductive logic was the rage. Or we get neo-theologies, designed to catch up political issues or new emphases on "hope," "liberation," "minorities," "women," or whatever else is current. Besides having a very short life, these "theologies" often prove to be thinly disguised apologies for causes which hardly need such a rationale. Whatever their momentary appeal, such theologies do very little by way of recommending Christianity; instead they recommend causes that do not usually need such extraneous supports anyway. There is a pathetic side to this effort that ought to be remarked upon; for it does appear that persons who do this kind of theology and those who read it are trying desperately to realign themselves and Christianity with the big and moving factors in our common life. The pathos is deepened even more when one understands the religious poverty wherein such schemes are born and the religious poverty that follows their assimilation. Unfortunately, before one learns the new theology, the world changes, and yet another theology has to be hatched.

Assuredly, this is not the way to do theology. For the people of the world remain there, a formidable foil for a Christian address. A conflict is set up in every heart when we note the existence of the nonbelievers and when we assess the strong spiritual forces in daily life which are hostile to the Christian faith. We do Christianity an injustice, however, if we think that the lively and widespread interests in various subjects, what can be called fashions, are the points of departure for addressing others about the faith. It is the very stuff of fashions not to last; and theology which gets an easy hearing will as quickly lose the public ear. Besides, the fickleness of human interest and taste is a good part of the human ailment, not its strength. The devasting harshness of God's love, which demands complete surrender, which fixes a chasm between Godliness and worldliness, between believers and unbelievers, between good and evil, is also the very reason why men are offended by the tidings that do not always sound attractive. Those who do not give God what he asks are also those who cannot endure him. A theology that is immediately attractive is often a poor introduction to the Christian life and thought. One must never entertain, therefore, a picture of a Christian theology as a net of causes and reasons, an intellectual proposal, which by constant assimilation of novelties, by continual adaptation to new circumstances, will reclaim the masses by its sweet reasonableness.

The real charge against so much of this journalistic theology is that by being adaptive and contemporary it also ceases to be Christian. It soon loses its Godly and supernatural content, and it all too quickly focuses the thought of Christians upon public affairs, massive injustices, and the crises of public servants, instead

of the plain matters within their competence. For the major topic
is sin, mine and yours, and this means the net of greed, pride, lust,
the love of money, the need for ego strength, and the dishonesty
that enslaves and thwarts us every day of our lives.

The question is still what theology actually is. I wish to insist
here that the core of theology for Protestants, not only Catholics,
is a divine "magisterium," which is the same from age to age.
There is a deep and abiding truth that theology proposes, which,
like a "de profundis," is a criterion and standard for all of human
life. Amid the mad whirl of our common life, this theological
stuff, this news about God and man, helps to redefine the human
boundaries, to tame its vagrants, stimulate the indifferent, ener-
gize the slothful, and give scope and promise to all those who feel
hedged in and even utterly defeated. Amid the highs and lows,
where ethico-political aims engulf us, where empires organize and
disorganize human passions so that we stumble in confusion, there
is still a great and level *via*, a narrow way, across these frightening
chasms.

Unlike the popular everyday view that theology must always
adapt and must always be contemporary, we must insist that
theology proposes something that is timeless and eternal. Instead
of using popular causes and ideas of the day and then clothing
them in the language of faith, the task of theology is to construe
those causes and ideas, their feasibility and truth, in relation to
God and his way among men. It is in this way that Christianity
stays always relevant, for nothing human is outside of God's
purview and dominion.

Most of us are in scant danger of being unacquainted with
what is happening in our world. On the contrary, with all the
subtle passions of modernity upon us, we are almost certain to
become children of our time. We have little chance to be
untouched by the winds of doctrine and even less to be unmoved
by the ethico-political energies that course about us. Most of us are
victims of the "Zeitgeist," not its master. So the theology of the
Christian tradition has as one of its principal tasks to instruct us in

that art of living which will free us from slavery to fashion and the danger of restlessly moving with the times. Nothing said so far, however, argues that theological formulations are timeless or that theology's language must be a series of formulae. The whole of Christianity addresses humanity with the notion that though heaven and earth might pass away, the things of God will be steadfast and firm. This kind of message requires that every theologian, like every good preacher, must mediate always between the varying passions of men and the abiding verities of God.

Because there are two foci, a changeable mankind and a changeless God, the theological teaching must always also consider the particular concerns and pathos of the day. What is indeed timeless must also be couched, in so far as this is possible, in the diction of the common life. This does not mean that theology must adapt to the popular psychological talk of the day or the clichés of sociology; but it does require that theology be stated in the vernacular rather than in language that is archaic, esoteric, or even excessively learned. Theology, therefore, must have a cutting edge which addresses the age.

I V

The task of getting theological teachings into the vernacular supposes more skill rather than less. It seems to me, after many years in the academic arena, that at least a very large number of people can be taught to talk the learned and quasi-learned discourse. Having heard students parrot their teacher "ad nauseam," and having read thousands of student papers on Thomas Aquinas, Augustine, Kierkegaard, Luther, and Bultmann—I am quite sure that the pedagogy is not very difficult nor the learning of their formal views insuperable. Besides, almost every church includes a small group of laity who can demythologize a bit, then give a once-over to existentialism and to the thesis that God-is-dead, and freely exult in a little free thought. If the trick were the

popularization of the last bit of the newest thought, then Christianity would have a most secure future. Vulgarization is not at all
impossible, given the popular techniques of teaching, the encouragement of voguish interests, and a modicum of gentle persuasion.

But getting theological truths into the vernacular is not plain
propagandizing, nor does it entail crude exploitation and behavioral manipulation. It is a good part of the task of preaching. For
what else is good preaching but vernacular theology? Here the
issues have to be very clear or we can easily suggest an irrelevant
converse—namely, that all preaching that people like and quickly
respond to is, *ipso facto,* relevant and central to theology. That is
clearly false. For what must be remembered, always as the tacit
premise, is that whether the people like the theology or easily
understand it is, from a Christian vantage point, a very dubious
criterion. On the contrary, the Christian teachings are, in most
cases, a bit against the grain; and consequently, ready understanding and easy assimilation are dubious. All the more reason, then,
for thinking about it the other way around. Theology tells us what
Christianity is and what and who God and we are. Because it says
what has been said before, for two thousand years, it might be
assumed that its formulations are now settled and the only task is a
given individual's absorption and use thereof.

Theology, however, is never easily understood; for God's word
is always directed at our self-evaluation, at our view of the human
prospects, and at our dearly bought expectations and wishes. All of
these and more get a brisk working-over by the Christian teaching. And what we most easily understand is what is congruent
with our standing hopes, with our ambitions, with the way we
have seen to our futures. This is how our complicity with the
social scene and the ethos of the world shows itself. We are in a
very deep and comprehensive sense "worldlings," and it takes a
breach of habit, of disposition, of thought itself, to recognize
ourselves as truly children of God.

I have already alluded to the fact that theology is, in a
restricted sense, an interpretation. But it is not an interpretation

that keeps up a restless change with the beliefs current in the world. For there is a sense in which the changes of belief in the world are not an improvement; nor are the new beliefs, simply because they are new and widely held, to be accepted as a new point of departure. Indeed not. Many prevalent beliefs, such as the notion that we share a new and general enlightenment and that human welfare can be secured by politics and science—these and more, grand as they might seem—do not themselves give a new content to theological teachings. Theology does not have to share their vernacular, however persuasive and gentle, powerful and promising.

For it to become vernacular, I do not mean that theology must adopt the argot of the age. Rather must theology be done by people who, scientifically trained and technically skilled though they be, must always be students of both Scripture and church teachings, on the one side, and the passions of the human heart, on the other. Those passions—the deep and long-standing enthusiasm for justice, for health, for everlasting life, for peace, for love, for understanding, for safety—these also permeate our common life. They are the subject matter to which all the great panaceas and all the shibboleths of politics, of science, of bright futures finally must appeal. Unless we can continually conjugate the human scene, variegated and diverse though it be, so that that aching human heart with its duplicities and deceits, vaguenesses and lies, will hear God speak to it, we will always have great tasks still to do. Not all the difficulties are theological. There are persons who are not yet ready to listen; and there are false teachings and disorderly ideas, many of which may have been, as their proponents always insist, acquired honestly. But theologians must, nonetheless, always remember that unless a human heart can be addressed, the long-term aim is being thwarted.

The vernacular here is not the language of regnant science or "pop" psychoanalysis or the "greening" of a nation; instead it is more like that residual language, that common diction, within which we all understand and describe the bitterness of grief, the anguish of hopelessness, the fate of the defeated, the cries of the weary, the hurt feelings of the neglected, and the elation of the victor. Most of us in situations like these do not speak learnedly, but we do speak simply and from the heart. We never cry, rejoice, scream with pain, or squeal with delight in the language of the learned. Of course, when we speak with emotion, we are not doing science or writing treatises. But we do often understand ourselves and others in such crisis situations.

It is the plain task of theology, whatever its point of departure, be it a glorious and extravagantly endowed genius of the past or a school of thought that sweeps all opposition before it, to move towards such simplicity. And if the theologians cannot do it, then they, in effect, are actually changing their subject. For one does not have theology stay theology if it is of antiquarian interest alone or if it indulges those who want to massage the dead. Once this is done, theology is no longer about the things of God. For those concerns of God are for the broken-hearted, the suffering, the weary, the sinful, and the little ones; and the natural medium for such concerns is the common diction of jealousy, fear, love, repentance, hate, and anxiety, of which we are masters already. Human life itself forces these words and their use upon us. It is part of God's mercy and grace that he addresses us where we are; and it behooves the teacher of these matters to think hard enough to extend that common diction to include the things of God.

2

What Theology Is and Does–Again

I turn again to the plain and hard task of saying what theology is. There is merit to the notion projected by Ludwig Wittgenstein that theology is the grammar of faith.[1] Calling it a grammar may seem strange and even rather forbidding. But a consideration of the role of the grammar of one's language might help a bit.

Learning grammar in the ordinary sense, i.e., English, French, or German grammar, may be done in one obvious way. We learn the rules and learn them typically "by heart." But as we go along, acquiring a mastery of the language, we do not speak the grammar itself but we say everything else in accord with the rules we have already learned. The more skilled we become in writing and speaking, the more does our knowledge of grammar inform everything we say and write. After a while we simply speak

---

[1] For readers unfamiliar with Ludwig Wittgenstein (1889–1951), it might be well to note here that he is a major figure in British and American philosophy of the past forty years. His thought is so different from most because he called a halt to the making of ideologies in the name of philosophy. He did not write a new philosophy—if one means by that a new metaphysics or a new morals or a new philosophy of religion. Instead, he tried to get clear all kinds of elementary things, like differences between names and concepts, and activities and capacities like "intending," "thinking," and "believing"—matters that have produced ideologies in the past but that he thought we had not gotten clear enough about. So his writings are full of brief but very powerful investigations of this and that—often matters that are almost commonplace. But he treats them with a difference.

grammatically without ostentatiously remembering the grammar at all. Our practice becomes intrinsically and naturally grammatical.

Something like this also obtains with the teaching of logic. When we first teach logic, we isolate logical forms and rules and teach them in an abstract way; for this is the only procedure we can follow. But our expectation is that those who learn the logic will not actually spend their lives remembering it; instead, they will, we hope, become logical respecting everything they think and say thereafter. What starts out being a subject matter that we teach, say grammar or logic, becomes eventually no longer a separate subject matter at all, but instead a practice, a "how," by which one does his talking and writing and thinking. This transformation cannot be effected on paper and cannot be done for anyone else. It must be, in a modest sense of the expression, a personal achievement.

More than this, it does in fact happen. Most people speak fairly grammatically, long after they have forgotten the grammatical rules. For it is as if the rules have become embedded in the speech textures themselves; and they are undoubtedly supported there by the fact that if you want to be understood, you had better speak grammatically. So the daily concourse of speech and practice tends to support the exercise of grammatical rules, if for no other reason than verbs better follow subjects, plurals go with plurals, or we will not understand one another. But the fact that people must do it according to rules and patterns, if they are going to reason at all or to speak at all, means that the rules can also be learned from the practices. Certainly, some capacities of speaking clearly and thinking with precision are developed because we are exposed to group practices in which those rules already obtain.

We can learn grammar and logic as a separate set of rules, or we can sometimes learn to speak logically and grammatically simply by conforming to the practice of those who know how. In either case, the closer we come to successful practice ourselves, the less overt our knowledge of the rules and the more tacit and informing those rules actually become. We finally become grammatical and logical in all that we say, even if we are hard put to state any longer the rules themselves.

I I

If theology is like a grammar, and certainly it is, then it follows that learning theology is not an end in itself. I am not denying here that theology can be learned just as grammar and logic can; most particularly, it is perfectly proper to do so. But there is the additional difference about theology that, though it is like grammar in some respects, namely, in not being the aim and intent of belief and the substance in and of itself (i.e., in not being the end but the means), still it is the declaration of the essence of Christianity. In so far as Christianity can be "said" at all, theology and Scripture say it. But what is therein said, be it the words of eternal life, be it creeds, or be it the words of Jesus Himself, we must note that like grammar and logic, their aim is not that we repeat the words. Theology also must be absorbed, and when it is, the hearer is supposed to become Godly.

The better and the clearer the theology, then, the more quickly the human heart will sing unbidden. For theology tells us what faith is; and the faith, when articulated with appropriateness and precision, is exceedingly good news. But appreciation and approval of the news are not the sufficient response, any more than hearty endorsement of grammatical rules and swearing allegiance to logical requisites are quite enough. No, we must become grammatical in speaking about everything else, not the grammar, before those rules have been really understood. So, too, it is of little use to be logical about logic when the point is that we are supposed to have learned to become logical about whatever we think. This is how it is, then, with theology—namely, that we are to become Godly in all things, referring everything, our woes and weal, fears and joys, past and future, completely to God's love and care.

This kind of transition involves each person's spirit. There is a kind of singular and corelike Christianity, surprisingly plain yet infinitely supple, and so inclusive that it can make Godly and Christlike, vulgar fishermen of the first century, sophisticates of the twentieth, Roman citizens and landless refugees, towering intellectuals and illiterate peasants. Just as grammatical rules can govern the enormous range of things there are to be said, so the theological stuff of the church and Scripture can also be instantiated in Godliness and a new life in the innumerable human host. In a peculiar way, the closer the theology gets to that necessary core, the more inclusive its grasp and the clearer its thrust in the direction of Godliness.

Theology is grammar in still another way. For just as grammar of a language is not quite an invention, nor do we simply make up our logical rules, so we do not design theology just to suit ourselves, nor do we invent it as we would a pleasant saying. The grammar of a language is that set of rules that describes how people speak who are doing it well and with efficacy. A logical schematism is also that set of criteria and lawlike remarks that describe how people think when they make sense. For those of us who are just learning to speak and to think, these rules are like prescriptions and even onerous requirements. But with the practices once mastered, the rules are no longer alien and become a part of the "how," the way, we behave. Theology is also dependent upon a consensus of belief and practice, that of Jesus and the Apostles, of the Scripture's teachings and the lives limned by its pages. Theology answers the question—what is Christianity? But it tells us the answer by giving us the order and priorities, the structure and morphology, of the Christian faith. It does this by placing the big words, like *man, God, Jesus, world,* in such a sequence and context that their use becomes ruled for us. And if we begin to use those words like that, with the appropriate zest and pathos, then we, too, become Godly as those earlier believers were.

I might enlarge my thesis of what theology is by saying two more things about it. We learn theology not by seeking God through the cracks in the universe, as if we were spies ferreting out his secrets or specialists with better instruments for catching him, either by improved perceptual capacities or by a finer conceptual net. Neither of these ways will work. We learn about God in the way a grammarian of language discovers the rules. He masters the language and assesses carefully what we all have access to already, our common working speech. So the theologian gets no new revelation and has no special organ for knowledge. He is debtor to what we, in one sense, have already—the Scriptures and the lives and thoughts of the faithful. Putting one's mind to that, getting it straight, so that one knows what belongs, what does not; what precedes what; what the concept of God includes and what it excludes—these and more make up our knowledge of God. God shows himself and is revealed in Jesus and the books about him.

This, then, is one of the two important things that enlarge theology for us. For this puts theology within the grasp of conscientious tentmakers, tinkers like Bunyan, lay people like Brother Lawrence, and maybe someone you know down the street who shames you with his or her grasp. Likewise it might explain why we who study so much, who read several languages, who argue so well, are often, as Augustine complained, chagrined to discover that others like Anthony take heaven by storm while we wallow in indecision and self-righteous knowledgeability. Theology is often done by the unlikely; in fact, if it could be coolly engineered and produced for a mass market, the world would long since have capitulated. But the world is still alien; and to a strange degree, God's ways are still discovered by his friends and not in virtue of techniques and agencies of power.

But consider one more aspect of theology as grammar. We have noted that the material is already there, the Scripture, the summarized teachings like creeds, and the host of practices, stories, and traditions that make up a Christianized historical content. For most, these are more than enough. The advantages of theology are like those of rules as over against the practice. Or they are like the advantage of hearing the rules of the game in explicit fashion rather than having to read them off the game itself. Surely the latter can be done—indeed must be done; for in the game itself we have both the criteria and the actual play, and we cannot get anything more than that. No man has seen God at any time, the Gospel writer warns us; so plainly enough, we are left with the game!

Those rules are like an abridgment and a more immediate access. They are rereadings that can stir us with their directness just as a grammatical rule can often frighten us into a practice sooner than leisurely exposure would do. And this is also the way Paul's admonitions corrected the early churchgoers and the way Luther's reflections on the Bible shocked Christians into a sharper definition of their lives. However, what Luther proposed finally was there already in the Scriptures, but it had been overlaid by neglectful practices and obliterated for its inattentive readers.

This theology of which I speak is infinitely more glorious, though, than the term *grammar* might suggest. For theology does not parse verbs, arrange thoughts, and conjugate sentences. Its matter is finally the whole of human life itself. Insofar as it is a grammar, it is more like the teaching that leads to a truly successful, deeply satisfactory, even blessed and happy life. This is why its promise is that thereby we make sense of our days. And there is nothing small or piddling about it at all. On the contrary, it is histrionic and magnificently dramatic, so much so that the rise and fall of empires, the tides of war and peace, the absence or presence of culture, learning, and material plenty—all of these are dwarfed in God's morphology and shaping of human destiny. Besides, one learns something from this divine grammar. We get a notion of what the world is, of what we are, and who God is. The fact that we are truly immortals, bound for an eternal destiny, and playing the whole game of God's presence—this is what the grammar of the Bible makes manifest. No wonder that it is no small thing!

Of course, we have already said that theology is an interpretation; but that does not mean that it is an arbitrary and casual refashioning of a subject matter to suit a whimsical and passing enthusiasm. Continuous redoing of the Scripture to fit the age is only a sophisticated and probably invisible bondage to the age rather than the desire to win the age for God. But if theology is grammar, then there is the task, always pertinent, of learning to extend the rules, the order, the morphology, of Godliness over the ever-changing circumstances. Just as a logician is hard put to discern the rules and extend those that we already know over the new things people learn and say, so, too, the grammar of a living language must always be open to the linguistic novelties and the sheer increment of vocabulary that is the fate of every living language. This, too, is a requisite of the theologian. His task is very modest and ought never to be overly praised or be used to justify indecision and the failure to be conclusive. There is, nonetheless, the responsibility to be continually showing that God's grammar is sufficiently flexible to take in the novelties of our changing life. And while it changes, some things also remain. Sameness in differences, likenesses in change, God's will in differing circumstances and lives—this is the Gospel's perduring theme.

III

But theology is still more. It is altogether too easy to assume that theology's form, its very style and shape, must be barbarously academic and formal. There are an unfortunately large number of precedents for this in the history of theology. So we have Protestants of the seventeenth and eighteenth centuries who wrote lengthy encyclopedias or, if not these, then in styles that are today as fascinating as geometry books. By way of parenthesis, perhaps, we might say that Thomas Aquinas's question-and-answer style, Melanchthon's dull and pedantic outlining, and Chemnitz's clear but deadly charting in prose might have been directed to special audiences that profited greatly thereby. But one has, I believe, ample reason for still thinking that it could have been better done otherwise. And Thomas's readers surely must include few who now find God there. More likely, having found God elsewhere, they find other things in the *Summa Theologica*.

Theology is interpretation, it needs to be couched in the vernacular, and it is still a kind of grammar that passes into the "how" of a human life. But theology is also a complex and many-sided subject matter. Thus far, I have been speaking of a kind of writing that is also about God, the world, Jesus, and the manifold of human life. It is not "about" these things, however, as if theology were totally a story written by eyewitnesses. Surely Luke tells us that he writes what he saw; but he saw Jesus and the Apostles. From that "seeing" and in virtue of other things, too, he goes on to write about God, salvation, and a host of other matters. It is as if in the manifold that he saw, he could also plot, like a grammarian, God's ordering of human affairs. He learned, in congress with Jesus, what *God* meant, what *love* required, what *hope* was justified, where *peace* was given. Insofar as we have knowledge of God, i.e., truly theology, we get it in the use and practices suggested by Luke (and other Apostles) around these and other words and teachings. Though we can learn about God from the Bible, we are also expected to become learners, to learn as we go, from living in accord with Jesus, and with Apostolic faithfulness in mind. Our walking by faith is also an ongoing learning about God.

This being so, theology must be more than a sum of truths. It is more than a compendium, and it is surely not just an encyclopedia. Insofar as it is put this way sometimes, its form is accidental. Theology must always move towards a present-tense, first-person mood. It must be lively and in such a form, at some occasion in its career, as first-person talk is in daily life. Theology, then, starts for us in this "about" mood—it is grammarlike and something like an account that we can get from others who have been there long before us. But we cannot absorb theology as simply the true account, nor do we really have a use for it in that form. For one thing, there is too much of it to believe or to assent to in an immediate and direct way. We cannot even begin to remember all of it, let alone savor it as it is.

So we must think of it in another way altogether. Indeed, theology is taught to us in an "about" mood, as a kind of third-person thought and language of Apostles, prophets, and our Lord himself. But to use it supposes that we translate from the third-person mood of being their knowledge and language "about" God to becoming my language "of" faith. This move from *about* to *of* is again not done simply on paper, nor is it done for another, *ein, zwei, drei*. It is all the more reason for saying that theology is not done best in scholarly forms and artifices of the learned. At best, the theological research that goes on does not quite issue in real theology—instead it prepares people a bit, at the most, for appreciating the real thing. It is like logic in respect to thinking and grammar in respect to writing prose.

Theology, to the extent that it becomes knowledge of God, has to have the form of personal appropriation built in. Otherwise, it is not about God at all but is only a history of someone's thoughts. For to have knowledge of God you must fear him and you must also love him. There is no knowledge of God otherwise. Without fearing him and loving him, one is not apprehending God but something else—maybe a concept only, an interesting story, a point of view, or something of the sort. Just as in learning grammar we must speak grammatically as the sign of understanding the grammar, so in theology, a great mistake and a fault in understanding obtains if we do not love and fear God. The grammar that is theology requires, objectively and necessarily, love and fear as the content of a person's Godliness. And the very knowledge that began in the "about" mood now becomes transformed into a "how," another mood altogether. One knows God in fearing and loving him.

There is room for our saying that the love of God and certainly the fear of him also have a language. When one reads the Bible, one discovers that every page is replete with the language "of" faithfulness itself. That is the true fate of theology—not to be repeated in the form in which it was taught, but to become transmuted into another mood altogether.

I V

The requirement, then, for those who handle theology, whether in pulpits or at podiums, is to project it with this in mind. That requires imagination, not just reiteration and a pedantic accurateness. Being sure of what was said and why is important, but only transitorily. The citing of a theological teaching also has to carry a projective thrust in the direction of suggesting the uses to which it must, not just can, be put. For without that, theology gets to be dull and misleading. It must be made clear negatively that theology is not to be believed as though it were ineluctable truths whose values were to be discovered by repeating them word for word and that often. Believing theology is different than that. I am not here denying that the acts of God stir the heart unbidden! And I am not asserting that orthodoxies have to be replaced by liberal teachings. Neither is this to deny that theology is cognitive, nor is it to deny objectivity in place of subjectivity.

But I say again that theology has to be projected. The literary means have always been metaphors, parables, stories, informal conversation, everyday speech, allegories, and a rich use of vivifying materials. This is not to argue for chalk-talks, buzz-sessions, or tea-groups; but one of the reasons these, too, arise is that theology is never perfectly done in syllogisms, arguments, and processes of verified reporting. The whole business of using theology as grammar requires also that we refer our nation, our world, our selves, our future to God. These very terms are dramatic and sweeping. It takes imagination to use them. It is as if the whole of life were God's theatre; we are all actors and he is the only spectator. Within that kind of projection, that imaginative construct, we begin to get the hang of ourselves and the world. We move, then, from saying with Paul that he lives no longer "I," that Christ lives in him, to start to live that way ourselves. This is where the positive projection of real preaching becomes theology in action. It works as it envelopes the hearer in the divine correction of disposition, of love, of orientation that is life-long.

This imaginative projection is the proper kind of popularization. It is popularization by vivification, not by vulgarization. Think of the ways it can be done. What if human life is an examination in which nobody can cheat? What if God has men in derision so that he laughs? What if the whole thing is like a divine comedy, with an exceedingly happy ending but certain conditions laid down for that everlasting laugh? Is the kingdom of heaven like a mustard seed? An unheard-of place with no crying? A place where lions will cavort peaceably with lambs? And what about that weight of glory? Are there any mere mortals about?

The imagination I refer to is not only an optional function which some will do if they have a stroke of genius or an ear for poetry. Instead it is the outworking of the language *about* faith when it becomes the language *of* faith. It moves from being like a grammar to becoming solicitous, personal, and persuasive. One cannot be solicitous without being imaginative, for solicitude demands that we have sympathy—pathos with and for others. We cannot do that unless we project others unto ourselves as God's children, as real and as worthy as we are and maybe more. When we lack sympathy, it is usually because we cannot imagine what it is like to be poor, ignorant, dirty, and hated. God's word forces us to disregard these attributes and see everybody as his children. But it takes imagination. That is why the commandment to love the neighbor becomes possible when we know that that most unlikely specimen is a child of the Heavenly Father. Those parables and metaphors are not decoration and little literary graces added to the hard facts. Rather, those strange imaginative projections are the very means by which love will well up in us and the grace of God grip us with heartiness.

The entire range of Christian commandments also demands imaginative deployment. We need imagination to make God's existence as our Maker, as our Father, as our Lord, and as our

Judge or King at all pertinent. For only a generous dose of "supposing" will supply the detail that will make motives calling us to the new action. We have to consider ourselves as pilgrims, as wayfarers, as warriors, as runners, as lambs, as subjects, as children, in order to make those moves in God's direction. The whole thrust of theology has to be in the direction not of finding something out—for that is only at the beginning—but rather of becoming something more worthy and justified. Surely we start with having learned something about what is, but we move in the direction of becoming something that God has planned for us. Imagination is the broker between what is learned and what is, in consequence, possible.

It is often said that theology states the meaning of the Gospel story or of the creeds and confessional pieces. But that is a misleading way to speak. For theology is not a more meaningful kind of prose than is, say, everyday speech or the words of the Bible. It is a mistake to say that we can have the Bible, on the one side, and then its meaning stated in another tissue of prose altogether. The entire picture is wrong; and every pastor and theologian must resist that plain and insistent request for a statement of the meaning. Just as the meaning of a piece of logic is not another piece of prose about logic but the achievement of logical acuity and accuracy of thought and inference, so the meaning of Jesus' life and death is not a theory of the atonement or an elaborate Christology. We are fooled into this, perhaps lulled into it, by the demand for meaning.

All the more is it the case that in Christian matters the formidable and somewhat angular character of Christian teachings, especially in catechisms and creed, doctrinal summaries and position papers, be thought about most patiently. We cannot everlastingly repair to one more piece to state the meaning of the last one, one more book to give the meaning of the previous, one more commentary upon a commentary upon a text. This kind of picture is all too easy to draw for oneself; and distressingly enough, it can be drawn to include most of what is already being done in many research centers, seminaries, and pastors' studies. This process should be cut off at the beginning.

The meaning of religious sayings like those in the Bible is not something that can be gleaned from those pages and restated in a simple way—except in rare circumstances. Once more, the continuous task of theology is both to say and to resay what are the rudiments of the Bible and of the faith; and this is its simplest and never-ending responsibility. Right here, there is usually no great difficulty. When people say, "I have heard that before and I think I know what you are going to say, but I don't know what it means," then we have a model instance of not knowing the meaning. Is it the task here to state matters in the language of the day? Yes and no. We have said that the diction of the day has its claims upon all of us. But there is another matter that puts the issue in a different light.

When we do not know the meaning of Christian teaching, it is also the case that we do not have any way to put on the saying, to make it work for us. The expressions lose their life, and they become dead in our mouths. The task is not always to revivify the teachings; instead it is to place the listener in another context, so that the words will spring to life for him. The church member needs to imagine himself as a lamb needing a shepherd; then the twenty-third Psalm can become his affirmation, and the meaning takes care of itself. If we can conceive of having citizenship in heaven, all kinds of rights and confidences will easily accrue. The point is that the metaphors and figures of the Bible are not sufficient to have exhausted the list. Any teacher of these matters will find a thousand ways to reconceive the role of his hearers so that they will discover their place, opportunities, and possibilities anew. This is how theology finally realizes itself in its correct form. The teachings do not have to change at all, for they are a kind of constant stretching through the ages. But the active pedagogy in which they are exercised must insinuate the listener into a new role; his self-evaluation, his subjectivity, his aims, wishes, hopes, desires, must be altered so that the grammar of faith becomes relevant. When the right supposal envelopes him, when he understands himself to be a prisoner, a victim, a sinner, a changeling, then the teachings will come to life.

This is how theology finally becomes something besides an ideology. For an ideology is a rallying point and a strident demand allowing no other allegiances. Sometimes theology looks that way, as if it were a rationale for a cause that is relentless and unremitting. But an ideology must increase its demands and live only by further exaggeration and ever more vivid statement. Theology, on the contrary, seeks a richer role, but one that passes totally into the life history of the individual, the community, the church, and mankind. It becomes invisible but all the more enlivening; it becomes so transparent that, like light itself, we never see it but see everything else by it.

V

I have noted that theology is an interpretation, that it is like a grammar of faith, that it includes metaphor, figures, and stories by way of a necessary projection of imagination. All of this is so also because it must be couched in the vernacular in order to be available and assimilable. Perhaps now we can fight a few of the ghosts that hover around and espoil the rightful dominion of the knowledge of God. That, after all, is what theology proposes for its hearers. We can become God's friends by knowing about him.

Somehow this is confused for a large number of would-be Christians. Theology looks like an option, one of the subjects that bear on important things but not with particular distinction. People think they have no use for theology because it is esoteric, for specialists, and way over their heads. Although this is certainly a mistaken notion, one must admit that much of what passes as theology is fanciful and technical and does not deserve a wide audience at all. It is divorced from the plain elements and words that fashion the Christian's faith. Certainly it is time to get theology hooked up once more with the clean breeze of God's grace that blows through the centuries. Then the outlook of this age or that is swept aside, as room for the Gospel is once more established. Theology states those simple "credenda," those rudimentary themes that make every age a part of God's great symphony.

There is no reason to excuse the pastor on the grounds that because he likes people so much he must, thereby, dislike theology the more. To those who say they are practical people and have no use for theoretical matters, hence have no theology, one must say that theology, indeed, like a theory, tells you what is so; but it does it in the interest of providing one his missing health of the spirit. Theology in the senses we have noted is not an option at all; it is the minimum and the necessary awareness of God, by which counseling, Near Eastern archeology, soul-care, geriatric services, and parish life get their correct evaluation and even their point. Theology is not one field among many; nor is it quite the same as what the department of theologians offers in contrast to other departments. Theology is certainly taught, and often under that very name. But the knowledge of God is also given to the pure in heart, to the fools for Christ's sake, and even to professors in theological seminaries and pastors and laiety in unlikely churches.

If we are not always sure of theology's source, we certainly can be clear about our need for knowing God. And God has not left himself without witness. The knowledge of God grows as we soak ourselves in testaments; the awareness of God is augmented as we let our moral consciousness grow; the cognizance of the Almighty is stimulated as we let Godly traditions form our dispositions and capacities. This is why theology has to be taught variously. The knowledge of God does not get moved from one mind to another in a direct and immediate way. What we can mediate from one mind to another is Luther's thoughts, the words of St. Augustine and the church fathers, the words of the Apostles, and the mediations of a systematic theologian. By themselves, these are not the matters called "knowing God"; but they are like a grammar and like a means with which you, the reader, come to know God. "Knowing God" is not done on paper. One must think about this by way of getting to know a person. The latter is accomplished by knowing all sorts of other things—what he did, why he does what he does, his likes, wishes, hopes, what makes him cry or laugh. After a while one can say, "I really know him"—though that "knowing" is not a simple act or certainly not a discernible occasion or happening.

Putting it this way, then, means that it is risky not to know others who knew God. We must always begin with the saints and the prophets, the Apostles and Jesus' immediate contemporaries. The Bible is our point of departure; and the tradition of theological writing, including less formal pieces in that tradition, is a kind of essential. Here is where acquaintanceship turns into knowledge, tentativeness into certainty, and obscurity into clarity. For the reader has to come to know God by knowing all kinds of other things first.

Nothing said here has disparaged the sheer "newsiness," the plain content, of the good news. Certainly theology is important because it transmits, not the knowledge of God, but rather all the thought and action within which knowing God becomes a possibility. But what a pastor must do at length in order to meet the exigencies of the entire range of persons who make up his flock, each member of that flock can do with a single sermon, with his own reading of the Bible and the raw material that is his own life. Certainly this is why responsible preaching is always directed toward giving others the access to God. God can be known and even enjoyed!

One of the hard sides of addressing others in God's interest is that most of us want Christianity itself to fit our secular and everyday aims and proclivities. Religious enthusiasm begins to look useful, if not as political drug to pacify, then as stimulant and tonic. Because the world so often suffers from a paucity of moral effort and from plain moral aimlessness, it is altogether plausible to urge Christianity upon people as a way of extracting that further degree of zest that will make for moral accomplishment.

Of course, there are always thinking people around who will provide a rather thin rationale for God in Christ being the author and finisher of such grandiose attempts. This kind of thing is often called theology but is instead a kind of religious ideology.

The moral tension created by this use of quasi-theology and quasi-religion is obviously dangerous psychologically if the sources of spiritual vitality to stick with such strenuousness are not increased simultaneously. Even more acute, though, are the gross misunderstandings of Christianity this creates. Part of the confusion we always seem to manufacture for ourselves we do in the name of theology, when we tend to rationalize causes and build up impossible and utopian schemes. Much of this generates that bad odor by which theology is so often discerned. The cure for that is more theology—a responsible theology—feeding upon those who have known God, and not just those who spin a web of possibilities and behave as cosmic judges on God's behalf.

All that I have said points us to the fact that theology must always be one of the ways that Christians learn to be on guard. For example, in days when Christianity is thought well of, everything claiming our attention is said to be a Christian movement. Theology is that knowledge that tells us, also, all kinds of polemical things. If only because one knows God and who He is, one knows a lot, too, that is not of God. Therefore, theology is always polemically poised; and it, too, like God himself, has to wound before it heals.

When we are prone to identify the Christian life and devotion with the sentiment that catches us in the throat as *Abide with Me* is sung, when we are most susceptible to a surge of emotion when taps breaks the silence, when we are likely to feel deeply as bombs burst in air and stars and stripes wave free, then, and especially then, we have to remember that these moments can all be caught up and are used by cruel totalitarianism, by gross and vulgar loyalties, by imposters and frauds, too. Then it is that the religion that tells us of redemption by the Son of Man, that puts a crucifixion in the center, that fixes us upon a God who sacrificed himself and whose worship must include the remembrance of all of that must be the center of attention. Only then can we say that such faith and such worship are the declared enemy of all who put the state, themselves, moral aims, institutions, or anything else first.

Think, then, about the emotions that are called for—lovely peace, lively hopes, inclusive love, a life no longer damned by anxiety and fear. God has overcome the world, and with him we can too. And the virtues that are called for? They are deep and pervasive, everything from a dauntless courage to a confident temperance, a fight for justice to the everyday works of love.

Theology like that tells us what is wrong and what is right; it becomes the way by which knowing God converts to serving him. Blessed we all are if in knowing such truth, we do it. Theology is directed to the essential spiritual core, our center of vitality and energy. Without such vitality we flounder in a spiritual morass and we die. The New Testament and the theological tradition, when seen from the outside, have an extraordinary unanimity about them, for they concern the same things in a myriad of situations and times. They suppose that we have no health of the spirit save through Jesus Christ, the physician of souls. Besides, the theological tradition shows us that human beings can be certain of these things, and, certainly, that confidence is also remarkable.

Theology, again Scriptural and traditional, will warn us of the frightful peril in which we all live, where the world has become deeply infected by sin. We are threatened by that contagion, the sickness unto death of our spirit, and it all happens so easily. The cumulative effect of sin is to make us captives by pleasantries and victims by easy conformity. Those striking teachings that make up the knowledge of God are also ways of training and disciplining ourselves so that we will not be taken in and will not conform to those standards.

The God we then learn about is no vague and general spirit of benevolence. He is pure and awesome, almost a terrifying holiness, whose presence promises the destruction of everything evil.

He is a blazing light of purity in a universe darkened by sin and foolishness. No wonder that there is a story to tell to all nations; for that God causes us to see that most of the roads we tread are leading us in diverting ways. There is slight tolerance of human divergence by God, for the stakes are too high; but there is a magnificent avenue provided by him with the most costly of means: the *via dolorosa* for Jesus Christ becomes the way to eternal life for all who will take it.

Surely this puts our common life in radically different perspective too. It becomes more like an incident rather than the main act. For its chief responsibility, weighted by theology becoming the knowledge of God, is to live this life as a preface to sharing the extravagant and timeless life of God himself. Here, then, our emphasis upon this life is shifted into a new key, and Christianity is, again, not to be treasured for its social implication as much as for its morally transcendent content.

If anyone begins to think that theology is academic and dry, it must be that the knowledge of God has been missed. What could be more exciting and more stimulating? It is as if there has been an invasion by the Almighty and a whole new quality of life can now ensue. This is no mere ethics, nor a new code, nor a more severe law. This is not new ritual or a more impressive religion. There is a sense in which theology itself, both the Scripture and the theological thinkers who are true to Scripture, tells us about an experience of life that is a strain upon the structures of the world. Finally, none of those structures will even survive; they will all prove to be mortal and will pass away, and only people and God will be immortal.

There is high drama here. Theology has a right to create fervor, to elicit a hymnody, to cause rejoicing. Because the world is like an alien background, there is also a way in which the knowledge of God needs imaginative devices to get human attention. The story, though old, must always be readdressed to all who pass by. When Christians talk about the many difficulties of our day as if they must wait for better days before Christianity can take hold, they will have to remember that the New Testament times were far worse. The New Testament leads us to the knowledge of God, and it seeded the faith in a time when there were no churches, no books about Jesus, and virtually no inhibitions upon slavery, poverty, suffering, disease, or the rapacity of rulers. Surely if there were no vitality in the seed, it would have perished in those hard days.

Nothing whatsoever is wrong with that old knowledge of God. We do not have to make it new. It is the recipient who has to be revivified and converted. And it must be that understandings are darkened and hearts are ever hardening in the mad traffic of worldliness. Sometimes the churches are no help, for they make theology look like a constitutional document for a clerical-ridden institution. The knowledge of God is directed against that. It is, instead, the declaration that we are as partakers in Jesus' life, death, and resurrection. We are also the pioneers of a new humanity, sons of light not darkness, and co-founders of a new kingdom of righteousness.

No imagination is too rich for such a story, no talent too strong. There is no historical tradition that has exhausted it, and no Gospel writer who can make it wearisome. Thus it behooves us to use what gifts we have, not to change the story, but rather to say it with freshness and with its plenteous attractiveness. And if we are weary of it, it must be that our understanding has waned. When that waxes, the words take wing again and theology becomes once more the Gospel according to God.

3

Theology and Belief

The issues of this chapter are two in number: first, to get at the tangle of themes which make us think that theologies must change, that they are implicit and must be made explicit, and must, above all, be the way to, or of, "understanding"; and second, to enliven some thoughts about being a believer. The chapter is engendered by the discomfort occasioned by hearing that theology leads to something called "theological understanding," without which the ordinary believer is deemed to be bereft.

I

If a student of esthetics or esthetic philosophies should be overheard telling a first-rate artist, "But you must understand the esthetic principles involved," most of us would at least smile. For it is funny and deeply incongruous to hear someone who has no art to his credit insisting upon the necessity of understanding esthetic principles, almost as a condition for artistry. In religious efforts, it is not so easy to laugh; in fact, the presence of an interest in very abstruse matters might mark the young person as a possible candidate for the ministry or priesthood and at least as very intellectual and serious.

In all areas where the performances are obvious and clear, there does not seem to be quite so much to understand; it is all right there! But in areas where the performance is neither present nor obvious, there we cannot speak so candidly. In the latter instances, "understanding" becomes highly internalized, very complicated, and often terribly abstract. Think about art again. It is often noted that esthetics is not a very widely nor deeply cultivated field of philosophy. I suspect that the presence of pictures, poems, compositions, and all the other things said and done make abstract reflection a little gratuitous. But in areas where the doings and happenings are few or even confused, there all kinds of things must be reflected upon simply to ascertain whether or not anything is there at all. Much of theology certainly must be so relevant, not because it illumines holiness and good news, but simply because it provides something, call it "understanding" if you will, when so little else is already there.

Christians are supposed to be faithful. Sometimes "being faithful" is a very vague matter for us. We have no visible marks, no stripes on our bodies, no hungering and thirsting after righteousness (at least not to speak of on an ordinary day), very little charity, maybe only a few feelings that look like cultural hangovers. And even subtle performances, private feelings, secret groanings—where are they? Is there any contrition? Guilt? Forgiveness? Prayer? It is no wonder, then, that there is a continual interest in a kind of reflection, a lot of abstract talk, about what in the world being faithful and being a Christian are. Maybe some things in theology are indeed "metaphysical," as so many students of both metaphysics and theology have repeatedly said. If that be so, it might also obtain that metaphysical urges are sometimes like the urges to theology. For when our lives do not make much sense, it is very tempting to have all the sense and wisdom in a big and inclusive scheme of reality.

For a variety of reasons, religion invites an almost continual effort at reflection. Of course, there are numerous things to know and to think about at length, some of them legitimately worthy. But is there not a great deal of theology that is idle reflection and principally so because there is so little to being faithful? When there is nothing to be, very little to do, and very little to believe that is the way of a Christian, then the burden has to fall on "understanding" and its correlative, "meaning."

Some students once explained to me that the Peace Corps had replaced the churches' social endeavors, that the government's legislation had now become God's principal action, and that community life was really the divine life. If this is so, one must think very hard indeed; for these arenas are not obviously one thing or the other—ethical, political, or religious. Maybe they have, nonetheless, a divine and theological meaning? Unlike earlier religious followers who would dare to believe that God makes even the kingdoms that rise up against him, along with the heavens and the earth to serve and to praise him, some contemporaries profess not to know any instances at all of serving and praising him. Therefore, they seek out in abstruse ways what serving and praising him mean. They dare not extrapolate from the small to the large, from the seen to the unseen; instead they look for "religious dimensions," for something religious in the secular, for religious "meanings" in current literature, in current social programs, and just everywhere except their own lives.

I I

Maybe this is what theologians are for—to tell us how we can be religious by doing what we would do anyway and believing what we would believe anyway. Theology becomes a gloss on the facts. There are some theologies about, very new and very relevant, by which we supposedly discover also the "meanings" that are apparently the gist of God and Gospel. They are found in our world where God is not apparent and where even the word *God,* if not God himself, has been discovered to be dead. This much is now said over and over again. Apparently this is what makes theologians want to do "ontology," where somehow everything can be grounded in "being" with profundity and, hopefully, with some religious pathos. Others want to do linguistic analysis, not because they really have some intellectual snags that need unsnagging, but rather because they do not believe very much and are, instead, terribly earnest about "meanings." Maybe the "use" of linguistic analysis will help; but *use* and *meaning*, contrary to Wittgenstein's careful and painful investigations, get badly misused.

Books have been written, both popular and technical (Bultmann's, Paul van Buren's, Bishop Robinson's, some of the new "ontologists" doing theology, much of Tillich's), wherein it is argued that the talk about God's existence is of no point. For better or for worse, this is mostly an attack upon a vague and traditional theism, less so upon the strange business of Biblical belief in God. However, according to some pundits, the ordinary man who goes to church and takes it seriously already is stuck with theism, even if he believes chiefly in God and Jesus Christ and the Holy Spirit. The theologians of this proclivity are telling us that even that plain fellow can no longer believe in God's existence and all those descriptions of his nature. This is what some authors mean when they say that the word *God* is dead, that it has no life apparently in those metaphysical schemes we call theism and supernaturalism and which were once described as "transcendent theology." And if life is gone here, there is no life or meaning at all, so say the critics.

This must be coupled with something else, allegedly more widespread and devastating. "The whole age" or "modern society" or "contemporary culture" is said to be against belief in God. So there are students of the times, apparently with practiced detecting eyes, who tell us that most if not all men are no longer prescientific. They are not believers, at least, in old myths; they are industrialized, empirical, tentative, skeptical, this-worldly, impressed by evidence, and repelled by things heavenly. Fortunately or unfortunately, depending upon how detached one can be, they are still anxious, dissatisfied, and occasionally fed up—all of this being enough to make "meaning" their goal. People cannot believe in gods, sins, God, or the devil, but they still need the "meanings" with which those were linked. So now the theological task, enough to make every Saul into a Paul all over again, is to isolate those meanings and somehow launch them into the sea of humankind!

This kind of outlook is very persistent and was by no means vanquished when the God-is-dead theology became passé. In a way, this is what went on in the early church, too, when the historical events of Jesus' life, ministry, death, and resurrection took second place to the supposed upshot and importance of them. A lot of theology has been directed to the task of getting rid of the reliance upon the historical account in the Bible. Lately, the emphasis is upon "ethics" and a variety of theologies which state "meanings" and provide "understanding." It is almost as if this outlook represents a permanent potential in human consciousness; for this kind of interest, theological and philosophical, is almost as old as both Judaism and Christianity.

Theology is reportedly faced today with the fact that the word *God* is dead, at least in the sense that it is no longer a word to be used for that which exists. *Post mortem dei.* We are told by so many today that God does not exist and that the word *God* itself is therefore dead almost beyond revivifying. Apparently it is like this. Most people, if not all, were accustomed by Scripture, church, and older theologies to think that *God* referred to something. Now, for very subtle causes, long in the making, we supposedly cannot think that way. *God* does not "refer" or "point to" or "represent"; for *God* is apparently not like that. God does not exist at all and there is no way to believe in him. But the point is that *God* (again the word!) can after all still mean a great deal, even if one cannot use it in the old way. Modern theologies, including Hegel's, Tillich's, Pannenberg's, (and perhaps Rahner's?), are ways to show us that the term has meanings galore if one will only think abstractly and in certain prescribed ways. As almost all readers of modern theology know, we can now do "Christology" in this new way, along with "history," "divine judgment," "sin," and many other of the big topics besides that of "God." Maybe there is still a *Geisteskraft* in language and culture;

in history and the future if not in nature; in Hebrews if not in Greeks; in the Bible seen in new ways if not in Cicero. At least these possibilities look promising for anxious theologues.

Things have gotten to such a state that sketching out a new scheme of such meanings is thought to be a positive and constructive offering. The argument seems to be that Christianity is nothing but a theology, for theology is the "understanding" of Christianity; and moderns cannot be appealed to in any way except through their understanding, and that requires a scheme of meanings. Soon all of learning gets involved. We know that genuine historical research should be endless and that small qualifications are the part of it that matter most; we have learned, too, that conjecture and surmises are the safest investments of thought and will lead to small but relevant intellectual profit. These freedoms of mind, guarantors indeed of objectivity, integrity, and criticism, under the pressure of the search for meaning also become now the causes of confusions, albeit very learned. For the temptation of the troubled theologue is to make everything count for everything, and consequently to lose sight of the precise and limited role of most if not all that we know and do in our genuine researches. In one sense of the word *theology*, there is no excuse for not relating it also to the business of living faithfully. If there is any merit to what is said here, it might be hoped that a penetrating simplicity and candidness, open to most men and not always a function of vast learning, can be encouraged, whereby an individual can also become his own theologian and mentor in faith. Otherwise, how can we explain the profundities of even the Scriptural authors?

"Was Christ really born of a virgin?" asks the wife of her pastor-husband, after hearing his sermon on the Third Sunday in Lent (in Olav Hartmann's extraordinary novel, *The Holy Masquerade*).[1] Her theologically modern husband, reminding her that

---

[1] Olav Hartmann, *The Holy Masquerade*, trans. Karl A. Olsson (Grand Rapids, 1963), p. 45.

she is ignorant of recent theology and too much a literalist
anyway, tries to explain:

> God has indeed revealed Himself in the man Christ. . . . It is the whole
> life of Christ that is the miracle and the miracle is not made any greater
> because one tries as formerly to explain how it happened. Furthermore,
> the explanation is only a literary form for the truth of the incarnation.
> For that reason one can use the archaic words without lying. One really
> means the same as the old biblical authors.[2]

The wife is very much like most of us most of the time. We are
"literalists," by which is usually meant that we want to translate
everything into something like that medieval world view of which
Santayana spoke so eloquently, making every biblical literary
piece a part of a very big picture. The husband-minister has had
this picture disturbed, and something very subtle and adaptive,
namely a new set of meanings, substituted. So now he talks about
the whole teaching and the main themes, and he refers his specific
difficulties to this more evanescent and somewhat abstruse backdrop of meanings. This much theology has done for him.

The fault here is not only intellectual and formal, though there
is plenty of that. But there is something terribly wrong with
thinking that every linguistic assertion needs explaining and
unpacking, as if it were incomplete and partial until placed in a
mutually enriching and artificial context of theological or metaphysical discourse. The matter is also painfully religious and
affects everyone in turn. For is it true that no one understands
religious matters except the one who has a scheme, be it transcendent metaphysics or another meaning scheme? Think of the
effrontery, too, of insisting that the teachings of the Bible and the
church must be considered as a whole in order to be given their
life and meaning. This ploy makes the conversational and almost
anecdotal character of much of the Scriptures almost a deception
or otherwise well-nigh pointless until more properly reconstruct-
ed.

---

[2] Ibid., p. 46.

But the terms are now rather clearly drawn. And in a time when we have revolutions of thought almost quarterly, there cannot be very much harm in just one more. For against the theologians who evolved a skein of discourse, almost a theory, which was said to be embedded in the discourse of apostles and all Christians, we are reading today a rich variety of criticisms of that theory. We are being urged to all kinds of vague theories of dimensions and meanings, all of them less antiquated, pictorial, and transcendent. Whether they are really relevant, free of offensive metaphysics and above all a veritable nest of meanings, is exceedingly dubious.

I I I

Our point is not to flail all the technical issues involved, though there are plenty of these. For example, Canon Alan Richardson thinks that the scientific study of Biblical language, which he very rightly believes is quite new and a startling development, also is the way to "discovering what such words as 'God' really mean."[3] Thus his argument is that the new theology of meanings, contrary to the older supernaturalism that continues to bother so many people, is really a kind of product of, not just a concession to, the age of science. In ways a little hard to trace (and which must make the nonreligious textual and philological students wince to read), a very modern Biblical theology, claiming to share in the age of science, purports to have been derived in elaborate scholarly ways from earlier and nonscientific uses of words. The fact that earlier users never quite described or used these meanings themselves is, apparently, beside the point. The thousand and one informal associations of words, concepts, and ideas with the uncharted course of human life that Scripture notes is now fixed by the narrowing and prescribing "meanings" of the theologian. Our issue is still, however, not these contentions, hard

---

[3] C.A. Richardson, *The Bible in the Age of Science* (London, 1961), p. 149.

as they are to understand, as much as it is the odd logic that makes it all so plausible.

Is it really because there is so little to most men's religious lives that something intellectual and explanatory has to be there to give even *some* substance, abstract as it might be? Or is it because even the language of the Scripture and the churches, along with everyday speech, is after all already theory-laden? When one author tells us that the language of the past, though mythological, was "only a medium for conveying the meaning of the past event," is this to say that every event had to have another medium declaring its meaning? Is this what theology is finally for? Does it only release and state the theory already contained in the simpler discourse?

Perhaps we are coming to a kind of summarizing point of the changes begun in the nineteenth century. There are any number of scholars who say that the new critical and historical methods which have made for finer discrimination and more accuracy have also made more sense of the Bible than did the old supernaturalistic and nonhistorical convictions about static revelation. But in some ways this is still a negative point, even rather old now. The new theme, not altogether done up yet nor quite vanquished either, is that Biblical scholars (even textual and critical students) can also create a kind of Biblical theology, in virtue of affirmative generalizations, holding the parts together in a variety of subthemes about symbolism, myth, and history. Perhaps this gives illustration to Canon Richardson's polemical historical claim: "In the twentieth century the last lingering vestiges of the nineteenth-century positivistic outlook have been transcended."[4]

So whether every man holds metaphysical beliefs may be a question, but the above-noted argument assumes that there is a kind of elucidating of what Biblical authors held, which elucidation is not simple reiteration nor a matter of discerning the outlines of transcendent metaphysics; but it is, instead, the matter

___
[4] Ibid., p. 135.

of explicating the meanings. Needless to say, this kind of thing has not impressed everyone; but there are signs now that this kind of elucidation, seemingly scholarly, historical, and philological, can be successfully blended with more typically philosophical and freewheeling kinds of efforts. Maybe some such synthesis will be the next theological "ism."

Perhaps it has been made clear enough already, but nothing said here has made light of many kinds of historical, philological, and textual inquiries. The difference, the quarrel, is not with research, whatever the subject matter. If people are ignorant, it seems most plausible and most worthy to become knowledgeable, however small the topic and however trivial it might seem to others. My point is a different one altogether. For a great deal of theology, old and new, has not been as much a matter of vanquishing ignorance and supplying knowledge as it has been a matter of speculative ardor and lately either an unearthing of hidden meanings or a fashioning of some extraordinary new meanings. My case is not against learning as much as it is against these odd conventions, old and new, by which that learning is used and most often misused. In conclusion, therefore, I sketch a couple of points that may remind us of proprieties and improprieties of what passes as theology.

I V

Concerning respect for the Bible, maybe it is true that people have read it using prescientific concepts to hang it together, or Greek philosophy, or this, that, and the other. Tyndale's insistence that the Bible must not be read always to document the medieval distinction between the religious and the secular is a case in point. Household tasks, he says, are as good works in the Bible as the ascetic life. Let it here be said that surely there are all kinds of misunderstandings of Christianity, of the Bible's teachings, of creeds, and of many other concepts, words, and parables associated with Jesus of Nazareth. Thus there are tasks for students of the

Scriptures, all kinds of them, for which every kind of exacting study might be useful.

But to assume that there is "an understanding" or "several understandings" still waiting to be expressed, lying, as it were, in front of the texts (like Plato's ideas in that famous story of the cave), still to be apprehended by great efforts—this surely is a mistake. Theologians then rush to this front—some from linguistic studies, some from historical, some from the no-man's-land of philosophy—intent upon the meaning. Maybe the text of the Bible allows this and that kind of study; so let it be done, by all means. But can we be sure that its meanings are missing? Of course, if the world, including the Bible, is like Plato's cave, then we certainly need all kinds of things, even meanings. Actually, though, is the text really so badly off? Its meanings very likely are not going to be found "in front of" or "above" the text, even in that other realm.

The trouble has been that, once bereft of one system of artifices of thought, we have been led to think that we cannot do or think anything sensible unless we have another. Having gotten rid of "divine meanings," we now gaze longingly at "secular meanings"; or having been deprived of scholasticisms, we now want ontologies. The man who says, "Away with those *isms!*" looks like a "positivist" who wants words without thoughts and the Bible without meaning. But so misled are we! For the situation is not like that at all. Even the Bible can probably be "understood" (in a certain manner of speaking) not by extending its language into other media, but by using it on one's own behalf to make it very clear to oneself how completely different it is, just as it stands. Instead of assuming that there are thoughts, deep and rich, for which the Biblical text is but an approximate and local expression, and which the theologian is qualified to unearth, let us really give honor to the text once more! For it might well be that we have to learn how to make the text become our very life-enthusiasm.

Surely people misunderstand the Bible. But "to understand the

Bible"—does that imply that one must write out a scheme of understanding, something called a theology? No, the purposes of theology are to help one to understand but not to be the understanding. Everyone knows, furthermore, how easy it is to misunderstand. For example, the word *grace* occurs in many places, including Scripture. So, too, do *world, God, truth, faith, teacher, sin, creation, good, love, righteousness,* and many others. Many difficulties arise from the fact that words like these are often known to us in quite different contexts, and we misunderstand very often by not seeing and using the word with the appropriate "how" in the right context. Now, there is good cause for thinking that the Bible is quite distinctive and that getting at the way of big words like those above is to see that they all fall in place, belong together, and make for a distinctive perspective. The role of theological teaching is to help one to see this or to do this, and then theology becomes "an understanding" by itself.

Perhaps we can now see how deceptively simple it is to believe that there is a level of meanings, more refined, clear, distinct, and transcendent, for which Scriptural words are only temporary media of expression. The temptation is to look in Scripture for clues to the overarching meanings, instead of pushing hard into the respective contexts and reduplicating for oneself the more homely ways of handling them. Theological training can well afford to force us to the differences that even Biblical language makes (though one has to be careful lest those differences be too easily summarized and written down once again as the essence of the Bible!).

It is unfortunate that the so-called theological revival in our time, Biblical theology included, has been primarily one more way to attract the talkative bright college set. All over the land these past few decades, it has been very easy to get audiences on behalf of theology. Much of this seems to me to have been because, indeed, the students and bright people were sick of naturalism, positivism, and all those other sparse and frugal convictions. Along came theologians, totally unexpected in such an age as ours. Were they preaching Christ? Well, yes, some of them indeed were doing so; but most often the appeal was not here. Rather it was the meanings, the generalized views, the invitation to having terribly big views that were so thrilling. Instead of the Bible coming in for either sober analytic and scholarly study, hard-nosed and objective, or for the painful reading by a person who was convinced that it might be bread for one's hunger or a lamp for one's feet, it became a matter of Biblical views of history, of man, and goodness knows what else. More views; and bigger than the psychologists', historians', and the new breed of philosophers'.

Is it not time that we think hard about these matters once again? And if our lives have been made anew by Jesus Christ and we want to wax earnest for him among others, then the Scriptures are still our tools as well as his cradle. The task is to help others to understand, but not by always substituting general views, supernaturalistic, scholastic, ontological, or secular, for the specific sentences and passages, but rather by using every means (including *views*) to get persons familiar and intimate with what those texts require.

V

We need more theology of a certain kind rather than less. But theology does not have to be secular because men are that way, nor does it have to trade in some current coin of the realm. There is an oddness in the fact that so much of the thought of so many talented thinkers in our day, not least theologians, issues in nothing more than an idle set of speculations, quite devoid of the pulse-beat of personal assimilation, despite its evangelical aim. Surely this is the place to reiterate that learning for its own sake is in order, even about the Bible, Jesus, and Jews; and one would be a fool to complain about worthy intellectual and disinterested accomplishment (of which there is a great deal!). But if theology is going to be done also for others, with the express purpose of making Christianity the evangel for the age and the news very

good, then let it be done; but honestly and well. Now it seems to
be done by a kind of nondescript speculative philosophizing,
crude and intrinsically dubious, save to the naive. Otherwise it is
done by what often seems to be an almost reckless use of
expressions like *meaning, mythology, symbol,* and *history* (and
there are more), so that erstwhile neutral researches will somehow
yield religious results.

More than this, the text surely must be taken seriously, but also
it must be stressed by the theologian (with the evangelical intent)
how important it is to use that text, and other things too, in order
to learn all the Christian virtues. For example, it is eminently
significant to learn to be patient and long-suffering, to learn to be
courageous and bold, to be hopeful and faithful to the end of one's
life. These things are not simply by-products of something else,
even beliefs or convictions; for we overintellectualized these
matters, almost as if everyone, all of the time, must first have the
beliefs of a transcendent sort in order to have these virtues.
Therefore, the hue and cry when the beliefs (or what we think
have been the beliefs) are criticized; for then the virtues seem
irresponsible and rootless, almost without reason or just cause.
Here again, we have thought too quickly *about* the text and not
enough *with* it, for it gives plenty of instances where these things
are simply enjoined and not invariably as though they were
necessarily consequent to very complex acts of belief.

One of the aims, then, of theology should be precisely to root
believers firmly in the Christian life. But this does not mean that
beliefs are of no significance. For one of the features of much of
modern theology, "post mortem dei" and in the post-Christian era
(that so many think already obtains), is that it indeed helps to
liquidate whole sets of beliefs. It suggests that we can have the
virtues and the way of life without the beliefs and the view of life.
Insofar as Christians are now suffering the blistering effect of
severe criticism of odd philosophical components, theories about
reality, and stray bits of metaphysics, it seems to me all to the
good. It is a winnowing that is quite healthy, at least for the

intellectuals. But the alternatives provided—no myths, no views, no beliefs, no God, but a host of meanings plus a little vague ontology and slipperly philosophy—are much worse.

Perhaps it is the task of theology not to be God's revelation but only to help people again to believe in God. Surely there are ways to come to this, but none of them is easy. The world has never made God obvious, and there is precedent for thinking that it is fairly well organized to keep most of us from acknowledging him. But theology can surely again show us how men come to believe in God and believe, too, that everything was made by him. It seems a little doubtful that the world around us is ever going to yield up some secret that will show everybody at a stroke that God is really the maker of everything. Maybe there is still a crack or two that men have not looked through to spy him out, and if so, by all means let them peer all they wish.

Meanwhile, there is still the matter of people themselves. For the issues of belief are, it appears at least, not strictly a matter of the quantity of learning one has, nor the talent one possesses, nor the extent of one's acquaintance with historical things (even others' thoughts), as much as it is the way in which one comports oneself. Therefore, the theologian has to be concerned with "how," for it is in the "how" along with the "what" that Christian concerns are enjoined. Seeking God with one's whole heart is no joke, especially if it might be the only way to find him. More pedantically, it might be said that even gaining the confidence that the word *God* can be used for something besides a meaning might be not just a matter of ontology or a clever move; it might be of a piece with the other Christian virtues and indeed so different that it might look like a major accomplishment if not a real miracle.

In fact, much of the Christian's confidence that there is a God who cares and loves comes, not from metaphysics, but from such odd things as the sense of guilt and the personal vicissitudes that guilt involves. And the concept of God, so rich and many-sided, indeed does belong within something one might call a kind of

Christian perspective or outlook. Maybe one can separate the concept of God from its tangled place in this perspective in order to examine it alone, perhaps to compare it with other concepts, and so on. But if one were going to say it was meaningful, one could only then be commenting upon what the word *God* did for people when they believed, prayed, worshipped, and perhaps tried to love him with all their heart, soul, mind, and strength.

If one wanted to make the word *God* meaningful to others, one would have to undertake some of the labor involved in showing how it works within that Christian perspective. It seems unlikely that the word will ever work any other way, for that's the way it gets its meaning. If Kant or Plato, Huxley or your neighbor uses *God* to explain some physics, or fill a need for an idea, or just plainly in vain, it surely is the task of a theologian to show that this is not the Christian word *God*. Certainly this is a task for a lifetime, if one chooses it! Isn't it a little too early, therefore, to give up on God?

V I

We began with the question whether much of this skeptical "meaning" theology is not finally the way it is because of a lack of religious and behavioral material to deal with. More than this, we might conclude that the reasons for the meaninglessness of much of the metaphysical theology might indeed be better scruples, clearer logic, more science, and the like. That is certainly what is widely said, and it can be guardedly granted. But it only explains some things, superfluous at that, which some Christians have believed. There is, after all, the whole range of convictions that the Apostles' Creed and the pages of Paul and the Psalmist also state for us. We are fools if we think that these are only bad metaphysics (of which there is plenty elsewhere). Much even of those pages will spring to life for us if we recover the rest of what went with those views. Everyone seems to have forgotten—in the enthusiasm for finding the myths and superstitions, bad metaphysics and prescientific cosmology that were probably contemporaneous—the fear of the Lord, the contriteness of spirit, the broken hearts, the pathos and felt need that were also there.

The important point to remember is that these may well be the religious stuff by which meaning will be once more brought to old words. And if the whole age refuses to move at once, is it not enough to do it for oneself? Besides, it will be altogether salutary to remember that words, even the Biblical and the Christian's words, do many things besides "communicate." Once one trains oneself—and then perhaps teaches others—to be open to the multitude of purposes served by that language (some conveys, some commands, some pleases, some stirs emotion, some entices thoughts), then and only then will adequacy be done both to the religious life and, simultaneously, to theology itself.

4

Scientific Language and the Language of Religion

Both philosophers and theologians in recent years have severely questioned the language of religious people. The queries have been many and diverse in intent; but withal and in the passage of time, a certain dignity has accrued to these concerns, evidenced now by the fact that they are referred to very honorifically as "problems." Almost any stripling without even the undergraduate's mastery of detail can tell you about the problem of "demythologizing" and the problem of "meaning." Though these issues are by no means the same, they are related. They both have to do with language, and they seem to occur together; most often they happen, too, to the same people.

Rudolf Bultmann, the veritable Nestor of a so-called critical and scientific study of the Christian Scriptures, has declared the language of the New Testament to be somewhat dubious. He says flatly that it is mythological. Simultaneously it bears a worthy story for needful men. The task of reading it for edification and help, of talking about it, and certainly of interpreting it with style and learning must be preceded by the demythologizing of it. The way it now reads and the way it is read (Bultmann seems to identify these for everyone save the critically trained and scientific scholar) are simply wrong. Professor Bultmann, a very learned divine, ripe with scholarship and Germanic culture, tells us that we can strip the mythological tissue of speech away and yet have a message and a language which is worthy of reiteration.

A point to be remembered about this kind of Biblical criticism is that it is directed against both what are conceived to be the ordinary understanding of Biblical language and the learned reinterpretations of it given in the recent past. Bultmann seems to be saying that its true meanings are hidden and that the learning to date has not directly aided their isolation. Right here, however, is the crucial point; for the assumption is that the text is already ambiguous, i.e., means two or more things, and that the text is what needs correction and interpretation. What so many people believe is intrinsically a matter of faith is for Bultmann an alien mythological addition. Therefore, all the tools of scientific study of language, of literary form, of ancient thought, and, of course, of earliest Christian faith are necessities for the recovery of the viable religious meanings. This very crucial conception of meaning and task will be scrutinized later.

Another and decidedly different kind of attack upon religious language has come from contemporary philosophers. In Sweden, Austria, England, and now in America, the philosophers have been saying unfamilar things about how and what language means. The criterion of meaning is lately a feasible project for philosophical disquisition and delineation. The thought has been that most language has "meaning," but that very few users of language are clear about the nature of meaning. Philosophers, who invariably thrash about looking for their subject matter anyway, have seemed quite happy with the proposal that they look at and describe meaning. It has not yet been decided publicly whether philosophers of this sort have actually discovered meaning and its criteria or whether they are up to their old tricks of offering a proposal under the guise of an innocent discovery. In any case, they have been busy discussing criteria of meaning and flailing several kinds of language with unbelievable abandon. We have been told which language is meaningful and which is not. Better still, it has been solemnly declared that there are kinds of meanings and that some language is cognitively meaningful, some is emotively meaningful, and some is altogether meaningless.

For the moment, let it be said simply that much of the language of religion seemed to come off rather badly. Either it was emotive and inexplicably helpful to sagging spirits, or it was really pointless and vacuous. No one should suppose that this account is exhaustive or even adequate, but it does point up the social situation where not even the philosophers have been the allies of faith. Where once the learned animus fed principally upon the natural sciences, now a similar animus becomes explicit and rather clear via a kind of philosophic study.

Intellectual change is certainly not altogether a matter of progress. And I, for one, will not concur with the widespread conviction that new and more learning adds up automatically to a net gain. Undoubtedly, progress is being made, but the immediate steps are often in circles and even backwards. Much learning also serves to confuse, and countless efforts have to be made to recover what was elementally clear and easy in an earlier time. Many of the contemporary criticisms of religious thought (and one could add ethical conviction, too) derive from learned confusions. Bultmann's thought is a case in point, for by arguing that much of the New Testament and much of early theology are mythological, he has suggested that the religious consciousness is clarified and enhanced, that religious language is purified and vindicated, by a kind of learned inquiry. To argue this way, one must have not only a command of discursive matters of fact, but also a kind of metaview. In Bultmann's case, it is certainly a philosophical view of man.

Professor Bultmann is one of the few men who has made striking contributions to our grasp of the literary and historical milieu of the early Christian church. Doubtless his kind of research enlarges and clarifies our historical consciousness a great deal. After a lifetime of such study, Bultmann tells us that the language of the contemporaries of Jesus was mythological, and that what they knew was already couched in a matrix of nonhistorical and cosmological and explanatory-like talk. Bultmann's researches certainly have been part of the attempt to recover the standpoints of the historical contemporaries and to know what they knew. But they did not know they were mythological and Bultmann does; and thereby hangs the interesting and dubious tale.

A major enthusiasm for the scientific study of religion, its ideas, literature, genesis, context, and forms certainly has been the promise that progress in such study might mean progress in the religious life, too. Most of us hope, as Bultmann and others seem to give promise, that critical and exacting study will concomitantly bring about that enrichment of conscience, that intensification of love, that communion with God which is our rightful heritage in faith. However, it seems to me that a consideration of the languages of science and of religion can only give us pause. A few issues will herewith be joined.

I I

All who practice scholarship and science know some of the things to which I shall here allude. But it may profit us a little to rethink and to resay them in a somewhat different context. Tremendous progress has been made in the past few centuries on a wide front of intellectual endeavors. Area after area has yielded its secrets, and today there is scarcely anything we can name that someone has not studied. All of this knowing has yielded that awesome accumulation of literature that inundates our libraries and gluts our curricula. The issue of all of it is a massive swath of language, the bearer of objective truth, infinitely rich, detailed, and extensive. Everywhere around us now lies the language of learning, waiting only to be taught and to be learned.

No one with a nose for knowledge can help being impressed by our huge accomplishments here. From casual impressions of the physical world, later codified by the Greeks, we have moved to daringly inclusive theories and laws about things terrestrial and celestial; from episodic and anecdotal chronicles we have now succeeded to reconstructions of the entire life and times of civilizations; from gross acquaintance with crude totalities we have discovered a host of invisible parts and particles, most of which could not have been even imagined two centuries ago. Both the scope and the detail are now greater. In addition, the exactness of measurement and the clarity of concept have grown apace. So, indeed we have much to celebrate.

In the past century and a half, a scientific study of religious materials has prospered too. Today, what frequently passes as theology is this systematic and principled study of religious materials. There is a loose use of the word *theology* by which we name the historical, linguistic, philosophical, and other kinds of disinterested studies that bring religious subject matter under purview. For the moment, the ambiguity of *theology* is not the issue—suffice it to note that the scientific study of religious materials is a genuine accomplishment. Again, the libraries are full of literature, much of it useful to assuage the pangs of ignorance relative to the causes, the historical antecedents, the social forms, the psychological motives, the linguistic expressions, and the reasons given by others for the religious life. And not only one religion is served thereby, for many of these disciplines and sciences have been applied to other faiths and cultures and even the comparison between them.

Since the early 1800s, European scholars have also made a discipline of the study of ideas. We can now make ideas, which ordinarily are the tools of knowing, the subject of knowing. The history of ideas is decently precise and certainly widely espoused. The history of philosophy is remarkably prosperous, chiefly because so many teachers think that the history of reflection is the way to teach others to become philosophical. The history of religious thought is not far behind. We can study today the rise and fall of concepts almost in the same way as we can study the fate of kings and the behavior of atoms. Of course there are differences, but there is still the overwhelming similarity to reflect about—notably, that we can command the convictions and beliefs of the past and the present in a cognitive interest. Anders Nygren's *Agape and Eros*[1] is a lengthy study of religious concepts in a neutral and detached mode. His studies are as scientific and as disinterested, even though they are about "eros," "nomos," and "agape," as numerous conceptual analyses familiar to historians of philosophy and of science. Students of "causality," of "fate," of "chance," and of "law" have long since shown us the way to descriptive truth about concepts themselves. Not only religious affairs have been thus studied; in addition, a host of other human activities have succumbed to an analytic grasp that now indirectly feeds our parochial intellectual interests. We have a scientific language about language, a language about ethics, another about esthetics, about love and making love, about dying, and even about thinking itself.

It might be said, therefore, that we are approaching the day when there will be a cogent and clear cognitive language about almost anything. Obviously we are pursuing here a goal that keeps on receding; but still the increase of knowledge is awesome, and the possibility of at least everything being known in some respect looks plausible. However, such a prospect ought to give us a little pause. For that knowledge will be mostly neutral and abstract in character. In addition, it will satisfy only curiosity, which is the immanent and immediate motivation for any kind of knowlege. It will not, as it stands, satisfy extraneous social demands or resolve other personal needs. We have to learn, therefore, not only the language, which is the medium of our knowledge, but also its proper use. That proper use is not easy to come by and to maintain, for an almost inextinguishable urge among the learned is to propose that the language of learning do more than it can possibly do.

Another feature is also worthy of note. The man who learns something for the first time usually does so with a great deal of

---

[1] Anders Nygren, *Agape and Eros*, trans. A. G. Hebert (London, 1932).

tedium and toil. Fortunately, though, knowledge can be taught to others with but a fraction of effort. Or, to put the matter more pointedly, learning at second hand is much easier than at first hand. By various pedagogical devices, we can increase another person's command of the language of learning in a variety of directions. We can correct another's errors, we can add to his information, we can clarify his reflection, and we can emancipate him from irrelevancies and confusions. Scientific learning, in contrast to commonsense learning or what is called learning from experience, has meant not only an increase in the bulk of information, incredible as the sheer mass now is, but also an increase in the extent of dissemination and use of knowledge on the part of others than the scholars, scientists, and researchers. It is a commonplace to remark now that the quantity of learning possessed by a young person today would dwarf that even available to the geniuses of bygone days.

Part of this is because of the increase of learning itself. But the creation of standard vocabularies and the writing of books (in short, the language of learning) has given an open sesame to what once was the right of the few. Much of this is summarized under the notion of making learning "objective." Nonetheless, all kinds of difficulties ensue. For the proper use of learning does not come as easily as the learning itself. The understanding of the learning inheres by and large in knowing how to use and construe the language of learning. Knowledge is, indeed, part of our accumulated social capital. It can be claimed anew at much less effort than it was achieved in the first place. Understanding that knowledge is another matter altogether.

No one ought to deny the enormous advantages, then, of being born later in time. But these advantages are almost exclusively intellectual. It is absurd to expect every successor to assume the anguish and to retrace the devious and painful means by which discoveries were made in the first place. Thus we can now learn at a distance from the originators, which distance is marked by time, difficulty, and even space. Learning is somewhat vicarious, and it is little wonder that hardworking figures in the history of science confess to standing on the shoulders of Newton. Another man's curiosity may have provided satisfaction in a well-conceived idea or an apt hypothesis to countless heirs. All of us can begin where another left off in a certain range of cognitive matters.

Certainly, then, we cannot deny that both the desire to know and the satisfaction of knowing find expression also in a distinctive language of learning. Such language is typically objective and disinterested, detached and neutral. These are its perfections and its guarantee of communicability and universality. One would be churlish to think ill of this aspect of scientific and scholarly achievement. For such a language about religion, about politics, or about artistic matters enables one to learn something about highly charged matters where passions run high and concerns are maximal, and to do so in fortunately nonpartisan and noninvolving terms. Thus one does not have to believe in democracy or its antitheses in order to learn political science, for ostensibly that science of politics would entail neither belief nor unbelief. So, too, with other matters of moment, religion, morals, manners, taste, and human responsibilities. One can see, almost immediately, why the thought of educators and students is so frequently charmed by the possibilities of extending the language in this "about" mood to everything important and divisive. Such an extension promises to make these significant matters teachable without the acrimony of partisanship; it promises a new mode of communication, one hopes in the interest of truth, that makes even the form of the language intrinsic to a scientific and objective grasp. The suggestions here are numerous and vast, but in theology the proposal becomes radical. The scientific language "about" religious materials—about the Bible, earlier beliefs, and a vast array of practices and ceremonies—is now redefined. It becomes the subject matter of theological study, and even the core of theology itself. It substitutes for another kind of language, the language "of" faith, which is the veritable content of the Bible. More subtly, another substitution is soon smuggled in. The kind of understanding we all can easily enough assimilate in this "about" mood and language replaces the kind of understanding that belongs properly to the "of" mood and language.

I I I

We seem to forget, almost continually, this distinction between the "about" and "of" ways of thinking and speaking. The sheer weight of modern learning makes the "of" mode of speaking, whether poetical, moral, affectional, or even commonsensical, seem too naive and artless for a contemporary person. Clearly enough, all of us can and do know "about" religious customs, rites, literature, ideas, traditions, and institutions. Whether all this learning serves a religious concern is another matter already noted. Most knowledge satisfies curiosity first and any other need only indirectly. What are spoken of as purposes may be several— the purpose immanental to knowledge is the satisfaction of knowing, and all other purposes are actually external and imposed teleologies. Part of the freedom cherished by scholarship is the freedom from what are considered alien and extraneous demands, be they political, religious, ethical, or even institutional. All of these things remembered, is there not still another way of speaking that is theology proper? Is there not a way of speaking that is a more intimate expression *of* the religious life, a greater clue to its province, a greater help to learning to be religious, than all the learning *about* religion?

Obviously there is this other kind of thought and language, one that is not of a piece or kind with our scholarly and scientific discourse, but which is not lesser for all that. We have already noted that the subject matter that we call theological studies in modern universities and seminaries is invariably in this "about" mood. It is called "scientific," ostensibly because of that very fact. All of it, be it doctrinal or church history, Scriptural or liturgical studies, shares a common pool of noetic categories and criteria, so that at least the disciplines are recognizably scholarly and controlled. The rules governing these enterprises are fairly obvious and almost plain. Theology, in this sense, looks like literary criticism and also a bit like other kinds of historical study, save for its subject matter.

The temptation is, in consequence, to think that theology in St. Paul's pages, in Augustine's tomes, in Luther's many volumes (and these are but a sample), is neither objective nor ruled—that it is subjective and invidiously unscientific. It almost seems by definition to be radically expressive, personalistic, confessional, illogical, and disorderly. No wonder it seems mildly partisan and a matter of bald advocacy. For purposes of illustration, one could include poetry in this context, for one has a host of literary critics who themselves insist that poetry is radically individual, that its meanings are private, and that it can only be understood as an expression of its perpetrator. So in religious contexts, it is easy to conclude that theology like the Apostle Paul's is also an idiosyncratic piece of writing, a bit of confession at best. Then it seems to have the values of a stimulus, but not much more. The "confessional" category itself makes such reflection seem immediately nonobjective, nonlogical, and educationally irregular. Admittedly, theology of this second kind is everywhere permeated by an overpowering religious passion. Such language is not neutral and dispassionate, though its evaluative tone and passionate bearing do not mean that it is incorrigible or fantastic. For theology (and other deeply passionate expressions of moved persons), in this second sense, can certainly be thoughtful and logical without ceasing to be an accurate and forthright expression of a conscientious person in the grip of a religious passion. Furthermore, it also speaks "about" all kinds of things and is subject to canons of true and false, right and wrong.

The language about religion and religious things is very much like the language about anything else, providing it is thoughtful, cogent, and exact. The neutrality of such language makes it a tool whose use is not prefigured in any way. The scientific study of religion certainly fails if it serves only a religious passion; for no more evidence than that is needed to believe that the study is not scientific. Pascal noted in an observant spirit that suffering was ingredient of human life and that the Christian faith was wedded to the suffering of man and God. Voltaire, noting Pascal's claim and the ubiquity of suffering, declares both Pascal and such faith to be misanthropic and inhuman. It would seem that the fate of knowledge about religion, when made most perfect, is the prospect that both the religious man and the antireligious man will share the same core of verifiable and objective knowledge and language.

Theology in the second sense is not so widely useful as this. Neither is it so inconsequential. If Muslims and Jews can share the same descriptive language about Judaism, if Christians and non-Christians can share the same awareness about the facts, ideas, and practices that make the Christian faith, there must be something else that makes for their differences. Granted that the language about the religion may be the same, the language of the faithful belongs primarily to the faithful. Its rightful use and meanings are limited. The language of religion is a language full of the love for God, whereas the language against religion is properly full of abhorrence. The same knowledge about religion is suitable to either the passion for or the passion against it. The language of faith, again in the second sense, is passionate, personal, evaluative, and useful for the purposes of being faithful.

But this sort of thing has been said oftentimes, almost by way of saying that it is nothing but expressive. It is frequently argued that such language could only be a clue to the psyche of its user and a means of self-expression to its proposer. This is, however, to elide a host of difficulties. For religious language in this latter manner is certainly not about religion in general, nor is it simply a clue in its hearers to an otherwise private and inordinate inwardness. It is principally about all the rest of things in the world, not religion itself. Thus theology concerns one's tasks, the world around us, right and wrong, the social scene, and so on. Whereas knowledge "about" is partial and fragmentary even when most perfect, the language of religion is inclusive of everything that is. The test of a sound moral and religious passion is whether it gives confidence and overcomes despair in the presence of the multitude of distractions that the world provides. The religious tongue knows, evaluates, and judges all things in the presence of just such a passion.

It is no wonder, then, that the language of faith, penetrated as it is with a consuming passion, is never relative, hypothetical, tentative, or experimental, as is the language of learning. The passion to win over all cannot help but be expressed in an equally distinctive kind of language. It must be remembered, too, that theology is both a reflection of the suffering of passional difficulties and an attack upon these difficulties. Thus, a governing thought is the religious universalism which affirms that every person needs to be transformed, to suffer, and to deny himself in order to find the happiness which is humanly proper. This kind of transvaluation of customary values and evaluations gives religious language and reflection its polemical bite. It is not absurd to suppose here a deeper likeness of mankind, a profound and fundamental identity, which gives moral and religious language its universality and scope. Then the language of faith has a different satisfaction in view than that provided by cognition.

The evaluations that seem almost instinctive and built into our common tissues of life are not easily controverted and are not readily isolated either. Most of us are but seldom aware of the moderate enthusiasms and minimal passions by which we determine our path and moderate our decisions. Theology seeks to change all of that by isolating those passions for repudiation and proposing a new and radical passion by which to live our lives. No wonder, then, that a new way of talking ensues.

Theology, it has been asserted, expresses an enthusiasm in virtue of which judgments and beliefs are articulated. Theology is not simply expressive, however, for it is also ordered by distinctively religious categories. This is not the place to specify what these are—suffice it to say that they, too, are part of the logic and shaping of the discourse. Forgiveness, guilt, sin, suffering, and joy are typical. The point of the religious discourse is in part served when it both suggests and testifies to a human life dominated and unfied by a master ethico-religious passion. All too often our lives become meager and mean in virtue of a hand-to-mouth existence, devoid of direction and teleology. In spite of the patent failures of every life around us, a bold faith insists that the way to a concentration of energy and experience is always open. A random array of happenings, a mad sequence of exhilarating and despairful moods, a concatenation of little hates and worse loves—these are a frightful caricature of what a religious enthusiasm believes a distinctively human existence to be. Religious categories give our language some tools for discourse about such matters; and what is a passion in our private theater of the inward life becomes the ideas and words of the most profound and moving religious discourse. Perhaps another way of speaking ought here to be preferred lest the confusions again abound. Instead of speaking of the inward and the outward (as if the inward were a mysterious process of inaccessible spiritual quality, the other more mundane and exoteric), let us say that the use of a religious expression is such that a passion is its context. To understand a religious expression supposes that a passion will also follow the learning. Or better, the language of faith makes words themselves part of the religious passion and life. The language of faith is not *about* the faith—it becomes another instance *of* faith.

Theology, in this second and guarded sense, gives bold expression to the principle that a life cannot be continually eccentric and bizarre. Theological discourse shows us an idea functioning as a pervasive and unifying force, enabling the spirit of humankind to acquire the stamp of character and the advantages of concentration. Surely the aim of the discourse here considered is quite different from the aim of any kind of learning about religion. Knowing has its teleology largely in the desire to know, and everyone must learn to use knowledge accordingly. Theology is not to be learned so easily, for its point is very clear that a dispassionate learning is trivial, especially when the point is that the "how," the mode of believing with all of one's heart, is the great need. Theological language has a definitive role, which is to intensify and to purify religious passion. This is its obvious function and purpose, never to be forgotten save at the cost of gross misunderstanding. Even judgments about cabbages and kings are enunciated in order to ensure the domination of this religious passion. Truth is neither disparaged nor denied, but the true judgments that theology proffers, like the judgments of the morally enflamed man, are made to incite, not merely to inform. A religious person is convinced that a kind of love, the love of God for all, will save the world. Failing to savor this love will mean that one is lost. Religious language is the interestful and passionate delineation and judgment of all things in the light of such a conviction. But it is objective and logical within that kind.

It is no mistake to say, then, that the meaning of religious language as here noted is a little difficult to come by. For we live in a world where all meanings of speech are hedged by opportunity, experience, talent, and conscientiousness. Whereas scientific discourse can be understood if one learns and is talented, religious discourse offers no such differentiating and aristocratic barriers. For understanding of this kind of speech supposes the willingness to acquire and practice the kind of passional sovereignty that the religious life demands. The language of faith is indeed public, but its meanings and uses are a little guarded—as one might well expect. The language of Augustine is still very useful if one is seeking the meaning of faith; for it shows what an increasing permeation by a religious passion will do in the everyday relations of life. If one is committed to a religious way of life, the ever-novel renewal and deepening of this commitment becomes the task. The aim of the literature is not simply, therefore, an objective delineation. Unless the passion were there in Augustine, the everyday relations could not have been so delineated; and if the passion is not there in the reader, the account will appear to be subjective madness. Personality qualifications become exceedingly important for this kind of learning and thinking.

I V

In this regard, it is appropriate to say that there can be no generic theory of meaning by which we can say that scientific language is more meaningful than religious language or that religious language of the first sort we talked about, the language about religion, is more meaningful than the theological kind we have just discussed. In fact, the whole notion of meaning is itself confused, and it might be better simply to say that we can learn the differences between ways of speaking and ways of understanding. The language of the lover is not necessarily a babble, nor is it simply stupid or emotive. For a great lover, blessed in addition with some skill at expression, evaluates the entire fabric of life as a challenge and promises in words never to let such insignificant events as war or death contravene his affection. The rest of his life might well prove a test of his passion. His beloved is not only heartened by his ardor, but she may be informed as to how the love between them will enable them to see and manage the world. So, too, is it with religious talk. However inconvenient and even obtuse it may appear, there is still no common scale of meaningfulness bridging it and all other expressions. This would make language too cheap a commodity, and we must protest such cavalier claims as presumptuous and vain. There are scales of meaningfulness within certain kinds of contexts and uses; every lover, every moral man, and surely the serious religious speaker knows that there are ways of knowing what is meant and whether it is meant, all of which provide a way of scaling the utterances as worthy or unworthy.

To say all of this is to admit that there are breaches in our speech. One way to express this fully is to declare that the logic of the discourse of science is not the same as the logic of religion.

Another way is to note all the different ways that we explain things to ourselves. For again there are many kinds of explanations. Each kind has its context, its occasion, its own province, and its own function, relative to a specific need. We are gradually learning that kinds of explanations are not necessarily incompatible. They are in fact incommensurable with one another, and hence there is no logical incompatibility of the radical sort. A scientific explanation is a particularly apt ingress to the difference between scientific language and religious language. For a scientific explanation discloses the constitutent circumstances of an event or a phenomenon and then the universal relations or laws by which these circumstances come to be as they are. A religious explanation is quite different in intent. Here a person seeks a justification for one's life in which the passion that is needful will find its correlatives in everything objective. The religious explanation is a direct use of pathos and does not resolve a dispassionate query or interest. Here a person seeks to know oneself and to explain everything relative to faith and to his or her God. So one can well say that a religious explanation is a kind of achievement and hence a heightened instance of the religious life.

The foregoing then, is one way to indicate what is meant by saying that the language and reflection by which a human being refers himself or herself and all things to God is describable by a different logic than that language ordinarily said to be scientific and scholarly. There are other ways, too, and a few of these will be briefly sketched here. There are, for example, no necessary relations between religious language and scientific discourse about religion. Knowledge about religion does not mediate faith. One can know more or less about the idea of God, the Bible, and other religious matters, and still speak or think irreligiously; for there is no transition from one to the other. Perhaps this is the reason that so much of theology and so much of philosophy, too, seem to make so little progress. Despite the vast increase of knowledge about religion and the incredible advances in logic, in ethical theory, and in certain other parts of the discipline loosely called

philosophy, there is still a high use for the classics. Those parts of
philosophy that describe and elicit the wisdom of life are very
much like theology in this one respect—together they do not seem
to depend upon the increment of knowledge for their persuasive
power. The criticism of views of life is really the criticism of the
passions. A singular case in point is the philosophy of Plato, which
has been studied almost unceasingly from his day to ours. Yet the
vast amount known about him and his ideas does not seem to have
aided or abetted the enthusiasm or composure that we call
Platonic. Another way to say this is that insofar as Plato expressed
a way and a view of living, he did so in virtue of a commanding
pathos; and neither reasons for nor reasons against that pathos are
adumbrated with finality in all of the scholarship about him.

The issue is even clearer with distinctly religious things. As
was noted earlier, thinkers of the past two centuries or so have
provided an inordinate array of religious scholarship. No doubt it
is more accurate, detailed, reliable, and transparent than what we
had before. But there is certainly no qualitative improvement in
the language of religion because of this. That we are more
religious than our unfortunate forbears is not at all clear. Neither
can we claim that the language of faith has profited in equal
degree. Is it now easier to believe? And, by the same token, is it
any harder? Are the conditions really not quite the same? Why do
persons of faith hearken back to Augustine, to Calvin, to Luther,
to Aquinas? This must be due in large part to the fact that these
thinkers had passion in addition to their genius. Whatever their
lack of knowledge by today's standards, they still had a firsthand
acquaintance with the pathos of faith. Certainly they had talent,
but there are many thinkers of equal talent; and despite their
relative ignorance, that alone did not render their thought about
God nugatory. Amid the quantity of religious scholarship that
some of us now must read, why is it that so much of it seems
trivial, pointless, and irrelevant? I suggest that the quantity has
little to do with the quality, and the quality of religious discourse
depends principally upon the presence of an immediate and

powerful feeling, a heartfelt joy in the new life, which comes not by scholarship.

Make no mistake, though. More or less knowledge does determine and decide our adequacy of intellectual grasp. Every man is debtor to all of those who make knowing more sure. Nonetheless, it is still true that the language of faith cannot be improved by much learning nor even imparted thereby. For nothing done by another can save our moral and religious efforts, nor can it shorten our pursuit. The language of faith does its best for us when it teaches which way to go, how to walk, and this in the footsteps of its progenitor. Though it may well speak truly, it never gives us the truth as does the language about the faith. It asks instead that we, too, have the pathos and the passion, and that we let the categories of religion gain their dominance in our daily life.

On this count we can liken moral and religious language. The person who uses either to dispense with the moral and religious life is a fool. The man who thinks a language "of" either morality or religion has meaning apart from the presence of a religious and moral consciousness is mistaken. The limitation of knowledge about morals and religion is that while it is (or can be) true objectively and disinterestedly, such knowledge is not essential to the satisfaction of a moral or religious interest. It satisfies simply a cognitive or intellectual passion and nothing more. The limitation of a language pervaded by moral or religious enthusiasm is that it serves chiefly as a mirror, as Kierkegaard noted a century ago. We use it to find ourselves, as a kind of test, to determine whether such a passion is really ours. Religious language may inform us, but its content demands another use altogether, at once more exacting and searching—namely, a moral and religious application to the responsibility of steeling ourselves against temptation and perfecting ourselves again.

All of this is said remembering the inestimable progress of the scientific study of religion, its sources, kinds of effects, causes, and what have you. The plea of these pages is simply the additional remembrance that to excel in one is not to excel in the other. On the contrary, many a simple and unlettered man is a better instance of the pathos of faith than the learned man, and even his language, with whatever its shortcomings of sophistication and style, can reflect this fact.

There is, furthermore, another and wry effect of learning. With the widespread dissemination of learning have come all kinds of difficulties of assimilating that learning. And the simple and unadorned ways of moral and religious speaking seem to be almost without authority and footnotes in such a learned day as this. A number of egregious errors then arise to delude us respecting our more primitive and immediate ways of speaking. People who engage in science seem prone to the view that there is a continuity between a scientific account about something or other and the moral and religious judgment about the same thing. I am not rehearsing here the difficulties raised by comparing judgments of fact with judgments of value, for this distinction is altogether too pat and too abstract to serve us. Instead, I am suggesting that even where differences between *is* and *ought* are not apparent (e.g., "God was in Christ . . ." and "Jesus was born in Nazareth"), there are ways of using these words that demand acknowledgment of deep discontinuities. As an illustration, we might say that from the most complete historical statements no one can infer or generalize that "God was in Christ . . ." This statement is certainly both true in a strong sense and also dependent upon capacities, feelings, and a pathos, so that one can see and know what is what about Jesus. Those capacities and that passion had been achieved in the Apostle Paul's personal history, and by that statement he is able to show why everything is new and different to him.

The processes of history do have their own distinctive categories and all kinds of significances for those who read such things. So, too, do the phenomena of nature. Without disputing the specific achievements of science and scholarship in the least, it still remains true that there is another cosmos to which every person has an immediate access; and this cosmos is the inner and personal life and the locus of moral and religious pathos. Lest this language deceive by its metaphysical suggestiveness, let us say more baldly that it is by reference to our qualified pathos that moral and religious judgments really live. But it is nonetheless true that moral and religious judgments are, in turn, about everything else in the world—about, in short, the large cosmos in addition to ourselves and God.

V

Now the argument brings me back to the issues with which I began. The claims that religious language is meaningless, mythological, or emotive do not seem to stem from a careful consideration of language and its several uses. It is not correct to say simply that science, religion, and poetry are different languages expressive of the same reality. The detailed reasons for this denial must await another treatment. Clearly there is a commensurability between a human need, a relevant quest, an appropriate satisfaction, and linguistic expressions. There are rules and uses for language relative to the range of appropriate specifics, but there does not seem to be any applicable general theory of meaning. It is not intended to assert here that science is inferior to theology or that theology is more meaningful than science. In fact, the discussion about faith and reason, or faith *or* reason, is, by and large, invidious; for it usually is invoked to give solace to kinds of obscurantists and people who prefer one to the other. The meaning issues, especially as couched by philosophers of our century, have thus far served to perpetuate these and other hoary and tired distinctions. There seems to be slight cause to favor the language of science over that of religion, or vice versa, if one is clear that these languages are incommensurable, yet meaningful. It is equally absurd to insist that only science is rational, while religious talk is *ipso facto* irrational. Again, though the reiteration may now seem tiresome, scientific language about religion (as well as about anything else) and religious language (which I have called theology—an expression of religious pathos and dominated by religious categories) do lack those factors which would allow the first to confirm the second, either to contradict the other, or either to replace the other. This does not mean that both could not be rational in a somewhat limited sense of that term; but it certainly would be a misuse of the canons of rationality to say that all language of a kind is either rational or irrational. *Rationality* is polymorphic, and we have to learn a greater rather than a lesser sophistication about the use of such a term.

There is an eccentric way in which these two languages do begin to conflict. If scientific awareness becomes a dominant enthusiasm and succeeds in attracting all the interests of a person, then cognition is a rival to religion. Scientific language becomes, then, the means not only to the satisfaction of a limited interest (say, that of the desire to know), but also the hungering and thirsting after righteousness. Millennia have been proclaimed often enough in the past and doubtless will continue to be so declared in the future. But when they are proclaimed as the fruit of scientific and intellectual discovery or as the meaning of new learning, then knowledge itself is maligned. This is why the best minds of our time have so constantly to keep vigil and to devote themselves to the task of eradicating the absurdities that the misuse and misunderstandings of learning bring into the world. We owe great thanks, if we actually take notice, to those persons who help us keep our categories straight. Not least do we owe a debt to the modest aims and accomplishments of analytic thinkers (and I am not referring here exclusively to the recent school that goes by that name), be they philosophers, theologians, scientists, or moralists, who point out the costly consequences of muddy thinking by well-meaning persons (that is, chiefly those people who are always trying to be helpful by deriving ethical and religious concepts from biological, psychological, and historical knowledge).

One of the recurrent reasons for the unclarity of the language of learned people is the very process by which they try to effect accommodations between ethico-religious concepts and language, on the one side, and scientific concepts and language on the other. There is no doubt that the proclivity for absurdity is on both sides. The claims about inspiration, inerrancy, infallibility, etc., certainly stem in large part from an unwillingness to admit that there are objective uncertainties and, correspondingly, to avow that there are some things, such as ethical pathos and religious faith, that a man will discover nowhere else except within himself. Not even the Scripture, supposing its truth, would thereby bestow inwardness, faith, and enthusiasm directly. Religious people, perhaps like morally earnest people, anxious for a newness of life, have avidly sought the phenomena of a distinctly qualified human life in nonhuman nature, almost as if what must define a person must be warranted outside of oneself first. Making the Scripture inerrant seems to have been a queer kind of warrant whereby the ethico-religious quest was further thwarted, this time by a rubric intending to serve the quest.

It is almost as if religious individuals have not dared to commit themselves to God and the good until they can prove that stars and planets, Jews and Gentiles, early and late, microbes and monkeys, Israel and Rome, have been subject to the same sway of God and exemplify a goodness apparent in this latter hour. The Bible (and its language) also suffers misuse, particularly when it is claimed to be the literal truth, almost scientific and simultaneously satisfying to our cognitive motives and our religious needs. Such is a kind of pious absurdity, long practiced by religious people both to secure themselves and to persuade others. Certainly an advantage that Rudolf Bultmann's thought brings is a little elementary clarity to such matters, not by his doctrine but rather by forcing one to reflect with his doctrine. Bultmann argues that the New Testament contains mythological stretches of discourse, and he means by this that the discourse is prescientific. To say that it is prescientific means, among other things, that the theology of the New Testament satisfied also a cognitive interest, that it did so in the absence of scientific means, that it sought explanations, and that these explanations were again in a cognitive interest and are now mistaken. This way of talking introduced more confusions than were resolved.

There is a kind of madness appropriate to learning, too. For is it not true that the New Testament demands that we retrace apostleship for ourselves, that we relate ourselves to Jesus Christ by repentance, love, and hope? Suppose one remembers this as one reads, and mitigates the tendency to read it all for more knowledge? My suspicion is that then the language of the apostles is not prescientific or scientific; nor are the explanations of the various apostles really of a scientific sort. And language does not mean something all by itself. Is it not madness to interpret the New Testament as though it served the abstract intellectual interests of its authors and its readers? The New Testament is commensurate with the life, use, and context that ethico-religious concerns entail. It fits a distinctive form of life.

Numerous other confusions of this variety could be cited, most of them examples of the fact that religious men and moral men have been unable and unwilling to let their literary expressions stand as they are. Just as the language of the lover needs no scientific explanation and no certification outside of the immediate passion, so the language of faith earns its own way and has its own meaning and use. Here we do not have a Lazarus begging for a few crumbs of knowledge by which to live.

V I

On the other side the difficulties are compounded, too. For men of learning are altogether prone to impute immediate and direct ethical and religious significance to what they do. These imputations of moral and religious meanings, for this is how they enter, are almost legion. In fact, the odd question that invariably occurs, namely, "Yes, I understand, but what does it mean?", often expresses that strange conviction that there must be implications, consequents and upshots that will be congruent with, if not productive of, our interests and concerns. The popular word among the educated and the half-educated, *meaning*, hides a mare's nest of confusions and misuses. Nowhere is this more manifest than when we ask about the "meaning" of knowledge. Very few people are content with the learned tongue as it is. Instead they puzzle out of, or impute to, that language a variety of things, and then the nonsense is multiplied. Much of what passes as philosophy is a peculiar kind of generalizing of scientific and cognitive language, or a synthesizing of it, sometimes a reconstruction of it, in the interest of richer meanings, more adequate to the vicissitudes of our daily ethical and religious needs. We need not pause long to avow that intelligence is a wonderful instrument and can never be sufficiently praised; however, this is not to say that all the problems of existence are problems of the intellect. Men of intelligence have talked so, most often overtly where all could hear, sometimes and lately a little more discreetly. While admitting the limits of knowing, we often let our speech beguile us into thinking that it is the meanings that are unclear. If we could think harder, reorder our learning, or reconstruct everything we know to fit an ideal language, free of ambiguities, then our harvest would be complete.

The theory of evolution, which is surely part of the intellectual coin of the realm, has been almost from its inception and again today interpreted as a view delineating a moral continuity stretching from nonhuman to human life. Because there was or is an erstwhile struggle for existence among the animals, it was and is argued that the animosities of man towards man, the antipathies by which wars are fought, the irregardless desires and heedless greeds—these and more are averred to be part of that same struggle. Surely this is ridiculous on two sides: the imputation of moral guilt to animals is inappropriate, and the justification of human ruthlessness by reference to a nature "red in tooth and claw" is an argumentative futility.

The language of morals states and uses an absolute distinction between good and evil. The temptation of many thinkers, including biologists, has been to argue that good and evil are stages in the progress of mankind. Such an interpretation of natural and historical phenomena not only suffers from generalization beyond the evidence, but worse, it suffers from the ingestion of categories not subject to cognitive and scientific interest and discrimination. Making good and evil subject to historical survey, as if they are more compelling in the large than in the small, is another effort doomed to failure. Moral distinctions do not arise impersonally, nor are they apparent to the disinterested intelligence. Instead, good and evil are emergents arising in the consciousness of an individual and are the sign of ethical maturity. Once achieved, the distinction is used everywhere; and it becomes a test of the viability of a moral distinction whether it is adequate for the mad array of circumstances and trials of daily life. Neither some things nor all things are, in turn, the objective source of the knowledge of good and evil. When men are conceived as burdened by their history of ancestral brutishness, then moral evil becomes an instinctive stirring, resident in the flesh or in bestiality. Surely moral evil cannot be identified with either sensuousness or instinct, for its language clearly describes the pathology of the human spirit and words, not the history or physical stuff of the man.

Likewise the temptation arises to use cognitive language to refer a man to God and the divine life. The temptation leads to a variety of circumlocutions that defeat the aims of science as well as deny the authenticity of moral and religious discourse. Sometimes gaps in scientific explanation are said to be the opportunity for religious speculation and acts of faith. Otherwise the specific nature of some scientific theory is exploited on the grounds that it has something essential to contribute to the life of faith and to theological reflection. Consequently, even some scientists have misinterpreted the quantum theory as if it were an encouragement to faith, almost to suggest that we were properly depressed by relativity theory. During the past forty years or so, a variety of students have been busy recommending Whitehead to our attention, almost as if organic and organismic concepts were evidence for God and the tools of theology. And it is not amiss to remind ourselves how often our anxious scanning of the scientific horizons is a response to all kinds of pressures to ground the teachings of faith in the verifiable teachings of science.

All of this distorts scientific endeavor while robbing the ethical and religious interests of their due. The language of science is circumscribed in use and scope. We only distort it when we make it do ethico-religious service. However, the long-standing interest in both matters at once has sometimes encouraged scientists to be relevant, and obviously the world is hungry for guidance, especially if it comes decked out as science. One result is that our languages become ambiguous because they mean simultaneously two different things in two incongruous and incommensurable contexts. A cure for this is simply to keep the language of the podium clearly that; likewise with the language of the pulpit. The same man may wish to speak both languages, but to make a single tongue out of them is to confuse and to compound difficulties.

The argument here has been that there is a kind of cognitive motivation that finds satisfaction in knowing about something or other. The language of learning is united hand and glove with this motivation and this satisfaction, both in the inquirer and in the reader, the teacher and the pupil. But the cognitive consciousness is not the sole determiner of a man's life. To come into possession of a moral consciousness is even more demanding. The story of how a man succeeds to moral and religious pathos is not an easy one to summarize, though both kinds of consciousness are acquired and are, in the modern psychologist's sense of the term, learned. The learning is not exclusively any one thing, and certainly the learning is not a matter of becoming certain of objective truths; however, this story again has to be told in other places and in other ways. Other motivations and other satisfactions are the stuff here. The language of religion, in contrast to the language *about* it, cannot help but evince usages peculiar to such motivations and satisfactions. When that language is about the whole world or even parts of it, one can do no better than assess the meaning of the sayings in virtue of a context that includes different motives, satisfactions, passions, loves, and all else that is the religious context.

5

Metaphysics and Theology

He knew what's what, and that's as high
As Metaphysic wit can fly.
                    —*Samuel Butler*

One of the easiest traps into which a reflective person can fall is the search for "foundations." Theology, not least in our day, looks like a string of thoughts that needs "foundations" if anything does. It is very hard to say what it is that people are looking for when they seek "foundations." Earnest people have sought to "base" religion on a moral "foundation," almost as if religion were an edifice, maybe an edifice of thought, built upon a groundwork or maybe on something below the ground. Physics was praised by Niels Bohr on one occasion for its "foundations" (mathematics), on the one side, and for its empirical researches, on the other (though what he meant was not clear from the ensuing discussion). The "foundation" of a new kind of psychology was once said to be physiology, and a recent and very sober student of human affairs said that modern sociology was not "founded" on abstract theories any longer but upon statistics. So here are instances of "foundations" and instances of confusion, too.

We all have been taught that it is hard to believe a report if it is said to have no "foundation," for then that report is also said to be "baseless." This is certainly one way of saying that it ought not to be taken seriously. With a "foundation," preferably of facts, of long study, of principle, of theory, or of authority, reports begin to merit attention. Reports are, in certain contexts at least, quite without "foundation" if they are idly made up, irrelevant to the task for which they were conceived, and not properly authorized. So rumors are checked by whether they have a "foundation." Sometimes we credit them because of who said whatever was said; but at other times this is not sufficient "foundation," and we look for something else. So it is clear that a church can be disestablished when it loses its "foundation" and basis within a society. Many old cathedrals and monasteries of England, founded before the Reformation, had to be refounded, reestablished, by Henry VIII. Social foundations change and sometimes disappear altogether; and the substructures of buildings sometimes sink, showing that what was solid and sustaining, even the natural rock upon which the walls were built, can fail to support any longer.

None of us "reasons" by analogy, though this expression is often and widely used. We often "argue" by analogy, and that is something different. It must be the case that we have argued by analogy both from institutions, which we "founded" by placing on a principle or an edict or a charter, and buildings, which must rest upon physical "foundations" that will support, sustain and underlie, to collections of beliefs and ideas. We are led by a metaphor to the notion that groups of ideas must also have "foundations" which are the ground, the basis, the support, and the underlying base. The notion of "foundation" is clearly a metaphor and a useful one, too. Just as a man would be thought a fool if he did not believe there were foundations for any and every building, so a man is now deemed a fool if he believes that there is no ground or basis, no foundation for, beliefs and convictions that are truly serious and worthwhile. So much is this the case that a belief or a system of ideas that is without foundation cannot really be taken seriously at all. *"Pietas fundamentum est omnium virtutum,"* says Cicero, thus giving ancient precedence to linking even the virtues with "foundations," as if courses of action and forms of character must also be properly based if not the basis.

Whether there are "foundations" is the question for most of us. The specter is a dreadful one—either there are foundations or there are not. If there are none, then beliefs and convictions must wither away much as Marx said the state would—namely, that without something to constitute them and to maintain them, without provision for support, they must fall. If there are some, then we must inquire as to what they are. All kinds of beliefs seem to have disappeared—and it is easy to say, though I suspect very difficult to make sensible, that they all disappeared because they had no foundation. If we do not press matters, we can go on as if something discriminating has been said, forgetting probably, or oblivious to all that is covered by the vast and inclusive expression *foundation*. Why, then, do your friends not believe that some people are witches? Are there spirits in the winds? Are not some people by nature inferior? wicked? moral? damned? Is there not a celestial sphere holding the stars in their places? When we think about all these things, maybe adding others like "born of the Virgin Mary" as over against "suffered under Pontius Pilate," we can easily enough see how many conditions are covered by "foundations."

Anyway, my point here is again to remind the reader of what he already knows—namely, that there are "foundations" for buildings and supposedly for beliefs. The fact that he does not know what they are for the buildings makes no apparent difference most of the time; when a building begins to crack, to sag, and then to sink, the work on the foundation is a specialist's job. Now, does it make a difference about beliefs, too? To whom? Do beliefs crack, sag, and sink? Some people say that they do. Furthermore, the theme is that the beliefs of educated Christians, plus those of educated Jews and Muslims are positively crumbling. But it is especially those of Christians that will concern us here. Commentators upon the intellectual scene of modern Europe have, long since, acquainted us with the supposed transition from the medieval to the modern outlooks. "The rejection of scholasticism" looks like the result of a breakup of an imposing structure of thought, and "the scientific revolution" seems to mark further devastation. The loss of faith in later times—say, in the nineteenth century—is said to be in part caused by all kinds of new things, new canons if not new foundations for historical, philosophical, and scientific work. Again, most of us have felt that the foundations have been shaken if not altogether removed. So, too, Tennyson's *In Memoriam* has a deep poignancy about it, for it makes us wonder whether there are any foundations at all. Indeed, that poem encourages doubt whether there can be any religious interpretations of life at all.

Of course, likening beliefs, not least religious beliefs (say the Apostles' Creed, the Thirty-nine Articles, or the Westminster Confession), to a building, as if both needed "foundations," is a little peculiar, after all. For beliefs, even those noted, must be believed, cared about, and put to all kinds of purposes, such as "saying the confession," "singing the Creed," or "informing someone what a Church teaches," answering questions like— "What did Presbyterians believe that was distinctive?" or "Can you tell me what I ought to believe?" The practice of comparing buildings (with foundations) and edifices of thought (again with foundations) supposes that those beliefs are separable from "saying," "telling," "singing," and other such practices—that is, it supposes that they can be significantly discussed without considering believing, singing, saying, etc. Therefore, they become like buildings—out there, to be wondered about, considered, entertained. Somehow even the truth of beliefs is thought to be a question better handled when they are considered that way—as if their truth is a quality added or subtracted, like a building's qualities. But the question is, nonetheless, seriously raised—are there foundations for beliefs? We do clearly have buildings without the builders; but there is an odd sense in which we do not have beliefs without believers. Without the latter, the beliefs are really nothing at all.

Today there is a veritable chorus of enthusiasts for work on the foundations of theology. The diagnoses are rather vague and several; and the prognoses are equally disquieting. The themes that are struck are rather familiar, however, in the long historical scene. Popular religion is vague, more chauvinistic than Christian, not well-conceived, and not quite responsible socially and intellectually. The churches with their avid members are pictured as grand but ill-founded. In fact, there are cracks everywhere. It is apparently thought that the serious people, usually very critical professors of profound subjects, have seen the cracks and have begun to worry about the foundations. Remember, there are indeed foundations.

Who are the specialists for God's creaking house? Are there any at all? Quite a few hands are up. They belong to those who will reestablish the edifice of belief upon something surer. And a couple of these proposed new "foundations" will be examined in the next pages. It goes without saying that most of the foundations are of a sort conventionally called metaphysical. By itself, though, that word *metaphysical* is not very helpful, so we turn to the kinds of research instead.

I I

There is a kind of "foundation" that seems too abstract and too general to count for very much unless one happens to think that words and beliefs really are in a kind of system. If our words are interlocked in such a way that the meaning of one word is closely dependent upon the meaning of another, then it will never do simply to learn words and whatever goes with those words. This is the conviction of those who believe in systems. Of course, meanings are mostly independent of one another, and that is precisely why one has to learn piece by piece, word by word, and, in Christian contexts, article by article, verse by verse, and moment by moment. But this commonsense conviction does not come easily in academic circles, so we return to the other and more captivating view, one that places our words in a role within a well-knit structure where there is mutual dependence. If theology is a kind of schematism, then of course there must be a kind of "foundational" concept for it, too.[1]

Here we have one kind of plausible research. For the net of language that is spread over everything seems indeed to be, if not our thoughts, at least the "expression" of our thoughts. Our thoughts, we easily come to say, mirror what exists. So, on the one side are the thoughts, expressed in the language, and on the other side is everything else. Thus we get *bats* and *balls, kings* and *cabbages, neutrons, men,* and *ideas*—all of them (and more) words that are used, we say, to refer to correlative things in existence. Words on the one side, and things that exist (maybe in various ways) on the other. Now if words are unrelated to each other, not least are their meanings unrelated (and how quickly and easily we draw a distinction between the word and its meaning!); then words are discrete and existing things are discrete.

A kind of reflection is long-standing here, however. For someone might ask, "Is there not an essence of all that exists?" (I do not ask this question, but only point out that others do—not least Tillich and Heidegger in our day). Suppose one looks at, or thinks about (are these the same?), the host of things previously noted. The theme is, I believe, that all the names and words for things that exist have something, perhaps an essence, in common. If so, that is "the very general and indispensable concept of being" (Heidegger). And if all the things (one must keep on adding to the "some" mentioned until you get "all") have something in common, something important, then the means of referring to "that" is by this very special word *being.*

Apparently this is what many people think is a real founda-

---

[1] A good example of ontological philosophy, making these points, can be read in the discussion between Heidegger and Cassirer, reproduced in English by Carl H. Hamburg in "A Cassirer-Heidegger Seminar," *Philosophy and Phenomenological Research,* vol. 25 (December 1964), pp. 208–222. The issues here are those elemental ones noted above.

tion, for it is as if one cannot get anything more basic, more fundamental, nearer the bottom of anything and everything. On the one side, that which we referred to as "things that exist," there is "being"; on the other side, that which we referred to as words and/or thoughts, there is "the concept of being." Every single thing, then, has something about it, if not in it, which is like that something in every other thing. The science of ontology is indeed a most abstract science, and of that commonalty ·spread. Some students of these matters are quick to say that a concept like "being" cannot be explained unless the word *universal* is also used; and one can at least surmise why that word *universal* seems a plausible gambit for explaining. For while the many things that exist seem to be often separated from one another—there is "this" King and "that" cabbage, "this" man and "that" lady, "this" idea and "that" idea—still the *this*'s and the *that*'s must be more similar than Kings, cabbages, ladies, and the rest. It is a question what these mean when they can be used so widely. But think about *this* and *that* when used for two ideas. The fact that there can be two ideas, separated as far from one another as *this* and *that* certainly makes plausible, at least if you do not watch out, the thought that though different (*this* and *that*), yet they must have something in common because they "are."

"Universals" have often been taken to be the something, the stuff, the entity, the meaning perhaps, which is in common. If one were to ask how you know a "universal," the the answer would be that you "think" it; for you do not "find" it, the way you find your friend or "that" man, nor do you become aware of it the way you become aware of the pretty girl on your bus every morning. But our point is that the concept of being is like a universal, only more so! For while we are hard put to it to say what a universal is, we tend to talk about it as though it were something we discovered, not invented, but discovered by some very subtle thinking. Our concepts, some people have argued, have these universals as their correlatives. But the concept of "being" has the "something in everything" as its correlative. Unlike the concept of "man,"

which has men as its raw stuff and the "universal" in all those
particular men as its specified correlative, the concept of "being"
has everything as its raw stuff and not exactly a universal in things
as its particular specified correlative but "being *qua* being." One
is rather tried in saying any more. However, all kinds of things
have been essayed:

Of such philosophies, we say today that they are existentialist or have
important existentialist elements within their structures. The term "existentialist" in this connection designates philosophies in which the question of human existence in time and space and of man's predicament in
unity with the predicament of everything existing is asked and answered
in symbols or their conceptual transformation.[2]

If "existence" is thought of, as above, as a common predicament for everything—men, birds, ideas and cabbages—that "predicament" is the specific correlative to the concept of "being."
Then the concept of "being" is the most general way of referring
to the *fundamentum in re*, the foundation in reality. But our aim
in alluding to all this is that theologians who have been much
troubled by the difficulties of believing in God and who have
sought, therefore, the "foundations" are much impressed apparently with the talk about "being." All kinds of permutations are
open to one here, even on the side of the things. For just as Tillich
continually notes the "predicaments" in everything that is, others
have done other transcendental deductions and come up with an
amazing array of specifications. My point here is not to discuss
these; for the validity of such arguments, transcendental or not,
does not depend upon what is said after one lumps all "existents"
together, but on the propriety, indeed, of doing this kind of
lumping at all.

According to this kind of thinking, if everything has "being,"
then everything is somehow linked.[3] Tillich speaks movingly

---

[2] Paul Tillich, *Systematic Theology* (Chicago, 1964), vol. 3, p. 216.

[3] A good example is found in Paul Weiss's book, *The God We Seek* (Carbon-
dale, 1964), especially "Religious Concepts and Sacred Objects," and "The Idea of
God," pp. 67–98.

about the ground-of-being, and it is a small step for him from that to God. The other side of the matter is the concepts. If all things are linked, then it may seem plausible to suggest that all the concepts we use are also intimately linked. Perhaps, some will say, our concepts are really a system; and if this is so, then the concept of "being" is an absolutely indispensable one. No one need read far before he discovers people who say that.[4] What it means to say that is not at all clear, and it is very hard to see even how to do anything about the unclarity. Something so widely said must, even if a mistake, be easy to slip into. All I can do here is to see one way in which we might slip into it. Our concepts, supposing that we "have" them in some manner or another, must somehow and sometime depend upon each other. If I speak meaningfully of r^2, a host of other concepts are involved. To be taught one concept supposes the others, for we often think about them as if they shed light or meaning, one upon the other. Therefore, just as everything in the world supposedly can be described and known in a variety of ways, the argument goes that every concept used in these processes already contains (involves, presupposes, includes, implies, means?) something more than is made explicit by the respective concepts. Surely this is obscure and a very dark saying; but dark sayings are frequent and besides are the prerogative of very smart men. For example: someone says "God the Father, Christ the Son, and the Holy Spirit." And the listener, very acute and very profound, says: "Does each have being?" The answer, fumbling to be sure, is: "Of course, what else? Could I believe in three Persons otherwise?"

The example can be variously pressed, of course; but I use it to show how often sophisticated people are inclined to think that words like those noted refer not only to God, Jesus Christ, and the Holy Spirit, but also to something else—namely, "that they have being." Maybe the person thus responding does not want to do

---

[4] This is the argument of Heinrich Ott in his *Denken und Sein* (Zollikon, 1964), in which he tries to show that the concept of being is essential to theology, and that by its 'help,' theology can be 'understood.'

anything more than simply insist that his belief is a very important one, but then his response could well be simpler, too. The interlocutor, the spy for being, takes the answer to be a strong recommendation for the interlocking character of words. For the words, concepts perhaps, do not refer simply to the person, divine or otherwise, but they are used to refer also to some very vague and attenuated meaning that all the concepts must somehow share.[5] Thus, some authors—Tillich among them, but there are numerous others, very abstract and philosophical—find that the Trinitarian words stand for concepts (sometimes the word *symbol* is used) that are incomplete and inadequate until the biggest and most fundamental concept of all, "being," is really put to work upon them.[6]

Thus, there is a great investment in a kind of systematization, a system of concepts, standing behind (as it were) the ordinary discourse. Whereas ordinary ways of talking, even about God and man, are anecdotal and rather scrappy, these more refined ways of speaking conceptually are more systematic and precise. The issue is, though, that if our speech is conceptual at all, then the question is what keeps the language viable and tough, solidly based, and with a foundation in reality? The argument of a certain kind of philosopher and, more lately, of several kinds of theologians is that there must be an indispensable concept—at least one, maybe more—and that concept must be correlative to something fundamental. And the concept of "being" has for a long while seemed to be the foundation, both to discourse and the net of concepts and to express what is common to all that is. With a host of variations, this move or something like it goes on and on.

The reason for stating all of this is to show that theologians

---

[5] There is a great difference between noting that concepts are rule-like, established ways of referring, for example, and hence dependent upon contexts, societies, ways of living, thinking, and explaining, and saying that all concepts are in a system. To deny the latter is not to deny the former at all.

[6] For example, Tillich says, "Whatever one knows about a finite thing one knows about God, because it is rooted in him as its ground . . ." (*Systematic Theology*, vol. 2, pp. 9–10).

who began to cast about for something upon which they could base the theological teachings, tie them all down, show how they start perhaps and how they mean (for all of these different things get lumped together in the search for "foundations") are frequently led to "being" and the concept of "being." Ontology seems to be a general way to show that what the thologian is talking about really does, after all, refer to something. The word *ontology* is, besides a neologism, worse than that, a technical expression by which some philosophers and lately many theologians tell others that they are after all referring to something. It is surely very strange to have to say that you are referring to something when you talk about God, Jesus, and the Holy Spirit. Apparently, what many people mean when they say that theology is without foundations is that it does not refer to anything real. The ontologist tells us there is a referent, a foundation for theology, and it is "being." All the concepts in theology therefore *refer*, though somewhat indirectly, so the argument goes.

When the questioner, the doubter of divinity, who thinks it is all words, wants to know what it is all about and asks: "Is there anything to it?"; the answer is: "Of course. It has its foundation in being." If this does not work, one can try the other side of the avenue: "Every one of your concepts already refers to being and you do not know it. Theology only needs to make the ontological reference clear in all of our language in order to find its place. Theology is the science of meaning, too." Or, to carry the matter to ludicrous extremes, it is proposed that ordinary religious language is symbolical and at least once removed, whereas theology of this being-variety is conceptual, explanatory, technical, and much clearer (albeit less religiously powerful and emotive).

There are many odd moves in all this. For one thing, it is downright queer to require an ontology (or whatever one calls this business—the word is used by Heidegger, other phenomenologists, Paul Tillich, and all kinds of others) to insist that the teachings of the Church are really referring to something, are after all meaningful, and are fundamental despite everything. Usually we do not have to say two things—first, "I am leaving for Paris tomorrow," and second, "*I* refers to so and so" or "the whole sentence is meant to be taken thus and so." Is the language of the Church different? Most of the time, language that has any genuineness to it at all does not refer all by itself anyway, nor does it have an accompanying ontological commentary which tells us how to take it. People (not words or concepts) who speak and write refer to all kinds of things, including God, and when we understand them we occupy ourselves appropriately.

Is the "foundation" of theology really missing, then? I suggest that the question is wrongly put. Is there no such thing as a foundation at all? Is it all mind? Think for yourself of the whirl of opinions, of vague queries and halfhearted answers. How easy it has been, too, to offer answers when no one has been very clear about what is missing.

Indeed, there is something fundamentally wrong with a lot of the theological talk of our day. Those who lament the change of fortunes, who say that theology was once meaningful to all kinds of educated people, but that it lacks that meaning now, ought to reconsider the issues. True, the role of theology was larger in the Middle Ages, and in Isaac Newton's day, and even in the European and American universities of the nineteenth century. Certainly it is odd that religion should still concern so many people, but that theology should have, by our time, become primarily a specialist's prerogative. Is it really the case that theology has lost its point, its referential function and use? Again we have to remember an elemental matter. If language is used referringly, the reference is not secured by the language nor by another ratifying "ontological" scheme; rather, the speaker or the writer does the referring. Reference is not a trick, a subtle bit of learning, or even a matter of insight. Most of us "refer" all the time and in thousands of ways, using words, gestures, and a myriad of informal and formal techniques. At one time, certain kinds of theology—at least a lot of languages about everything under the sun including *God*—had a kind of currency. We can read this kind of language in John Locke, Newton, Jefferson, Harvey, Leibniz, Pascal, or Priestly, even when they are talking about governments, the behavior of physical things, mathematical problems, and lots else. Whether all of this is religiously serious is a moot point, and it may well be that this somewhat loose theological talk was actually only another informal scheme, common to educated people, within which they could easily enough refer to other things, too. In the thinkers noted above, and in popular literature of the same period, the concept of God was used referringly, almost as if everything else could be related to a divine presence. The intellectual history here noted might well be an indication of a confusion, too. For the language "of" faith was intertwined with the new and emerging language "about" natural things. When the theological language began to disappear, it might have been only that a language in the "about" mood was coming into existence. Thus more specific ways of referring to a host of things, without the God-idea, were developed. This may well be a net gain for everyone, including religious people. Or is it a serious loss to religious people?

The notion that a concept, especially one like that of "being," will restore vitality to a kind of general theology seems to me downright ludicrous. The Roman Catholic theologian Karl Rahner seems infatuated with this possibility (following Heidegger), and there are numerous others, too. Perhaps this is believed because something else besides "reference" and "a foundation in reality" is at stake—namely, the meaning of the discourse, supposedly "as a whole." Because just as everything has "being" (in senses very obscure and surely confounding to consider—take "being" away and what would you have?), so all theological words, considered together, are said to have special and important meanings given them if and when the "being-reference" is duly thought. But this is only another permutation on the notion that there is a "foundation"—an abstract and general "foundation"—for theology and everything else; and it will have to be otherwise discussed.

To state the issues like this is, I hope, to expose the entire effort. This kind of move, heavily freighted with portentous language and a kind of evangelical seriousness, proposed by persons often earnest and obscurely profound, is finally only possible to take seriously if one does not know exactly what is going on. Anyway, if the best part of theological language is thus disguised, it would be better to state it directly. But is there a way to state it directly? What is being said?

There is, however, another and more tangible way to search out foundations. This, in the interests of much theology and also some other views of life and popular philosophies, is the search for facts. Not least of the ways to make certain outlooks (as well as skeins of more elaborate discourse) appear respectable is to insist that "facts" are the basis and the foundation. To this we now turn.

III

The reputation accruing to much philosophy and theology, at least of the encompassing sort, is that they are systematic. Since the nineteenth century, much of theology has been described as just that, partly to distinguish it from historical accounts and partly to say that it was not dogmatic and authoritarian. But more than this is at stake, too; for theology has been conceived as a kind of homogeneous domain in which certain relations and rules of logic would therefore hold. With a certain modicum of success, theologies do loom rather large in this rare economy of systems. With the collapse of so many other systems, philosophical, economic, and political, the theological systems are among the few that are even being perpetrated at all. Theologies, like any other discourse that proposes to be systematic, are only viable if the chains of inference that lead from one topic to another are relatively strict. Anyone who peers into Schleiermacher's pages cannot help but notice how tight some of his discourse is, even though his notion of absolute dependence is so trivial; and even Paul Tillich's three-volumed *Systematic Theology*, despite many references to things in the world, imparts a homogeneity to everything talked about that makes it intellectually attractive and a mark of a certain kind of intellectual power. This sort of thing can be said about Marx's writings on political economy, matched perhaps only by Joan Robinson's "systematic" grasp in these latter times.

There is no reason to deny this side of the systematic interest. Neither can it be denied that theologians are among the few thinkers who are satisfying the craving for this homogeneous thinking and talking. Logically it might be described something like this: as though systematic theologies (and philosophies) were aiming at perfectly formalized schemes that would be conceptually homogeneous—where the relations between concepts could be known—and yet where the reference would be to the world, God, and all things. Of course, a very big order! The concept of being, if it could be shown to be indispensable, would apparently be the link, the foundation, the *in re* point.

There have been numerous criticisms of such endeavors through the centuries. Sometimes religious fervor, protests against abstract reflection; a respect for the Bible, an empirical drive, these and more have sounded the alarm. And there have been, consequently, theologies like Luther's, about almost everything but not formal; like Calvin's, related to a few things but not very abstract; and like Wesley's, rather *ad hoc* and addressing old truths to new situations. But also during the nineteenth century, along with the "systems," a cleft seems to have developed that is very broad today between a kind of factual theological interest already noted and that typical of systematicians.

For better or for worse, there are those who think there must be some facts that are fundamental and the foundation for the faith. Now it is old hat, of course, to recite all these things; but "Was there a Jesus or was there not?" seems very important indeed. "Did God make the world or didn't He?" we can hear someone say—"Isn't it a question of fact?" Is it a fact that Moses lived and went up on that mountain to get those tablets? Is it a fact that Noah lived so long, that Jesus rose from the dead, that

Paul had that remarkable experience on the road to Damascus, that God is a Spirit, that a man reaps what he sows, that Cretans are liars, or that there is a hell to go to?

The skein of theological concepts and statements, whether systematic or not, can so easily be questioned by "Is it a fact that . . .?" One can understand, too, how the question becomes fundamental. For if there is nothing "factual," then our habits easily lead us to say there are only illusions, opinions, interpretations, theories, speculations, generalizations, fancies, fiction, art, etc. Thus the concept of "fact" has loomed very large indeed as historical and critical studies upon texts, figures, and institutions have prospered during the past decades. For "fact" has been made to seem very formidable and desirable. This we can see easily enough from all the words modifying facts: *scientific, cold, historical, the, clear, solid, simple, ultimate, indubitable, undeniable, plain, stated, atomic, indestructible, irreducible,* and more.

So relentless and brutish, so cold and uninviting have "facts" sometimes loomed that questions of "value" have often looked more "foundational" than questions of "fact," not least to men of affairs and religious teachers. In earlier times, not so much recently, matters of law seemed more inclusive of Christian interests than did matters of fact, whereas recently "matters of language" have covered a host of concerns—philosophical (to the disgust of people like Bertrand Russell) and theological (to the surprise of most)—that formerly were stuck to "matters of fact." Withal, the strong tide for concern with the facts promises to be with us for a long time, if for no other reason than that both the Old and the New Testaments invite scholars into the research for the facts. Of course, everybody knows that if one is to be religious at all, he has also to obey God's commandments, follow his Lord, and love his neighbor—all of these are also solicited by those books. But so insidious is the doubt and so thorough the dismay that at least the bright people seem to think that they have to know first what the facts are. Thus the facts—whether there was a Jesus at all, whether the commands are God's or only inventions of the ancient upper classes—these, we find ourselves saying, must be ascertained before any following or obedience is contemplated.

The more insistent that theologians have been upon the historical and veridical character of the Bible and of theology, the more necessary it has been to become clear on the "facts." For concepts like "historical," "truth" and "fact" seem minimal, rock-bottom, and almost primitive and underived. Everybody claims to know what they mean—they seem to be the very furniture of our everyday talk. Those of us whose vocation is sometimes to think for others, as well as for ourselves, are strongly inclined to assume that facts are facts, the minimal elements of our knowledge, from which we can legitimately and rationally construct an account of anything appropriate. If theology is to be the truth about God and the world, surely, we say, it must start from a fact. If factual, then what are the facts? Ay, there is the rub! Who is to say?

Again we have to invoke some pictures that make this question appear a pertinent one. For to be without the facts is indeed like being without the *in re;* or we might say that it is like being a tree without roots, only more serious than that—for some trees, like those in our homes at Christmas, are quite all right for a considerable period. It is as though theological sayings were airborne with no connection with the ground; about something, but one is not quite clear what; an edifice of thought with no foundation other than someone's putting it together. When contemporary students of religion lament the situation of theology today, they seem convinced that it must appear authentic, worthy of being taken seriously, and pertinent to modern men only if some kind of connection can be made between the theology and reality via facts.

Perhaps it is because theology is likened to a kind of blanketing discourse, something that covers God, world, and men, and tells the truth about them. If theology is conceived that way, then there must be some ways to match the things talked about and the talk itself. "Facts" seem to fit the requirements. Are there *any* facts? Mind you, because the Christians (and some Jews) have already insisted that Christianity (and Judaism) is historical (this term, too, is difficult to pin down), it becomes plausible to say that there must be *some* historical facts.

This seems very promising. With the guidance of the concept "fact," whole groups of scholars have been directed to researches for the facts as the foundation of theology. Sometimes we have heard the new theologies praised for being "historical," "genuinely Biblical," and "less dogmatic, more factual." But the point is a delicate one, for there are all kinds of researches—literary, historical, and otherwise—that have "the facts" as their goal and aim. And no criticism is intended, whether these are the researches of scholars on Greeks, Jews, Christians, Hindus, or Hittites. There are all kinds of facts and all kinds of concepts of fact. But the difficulty here is that what is legitimate—namely, a resolute search for this or that—lends its genuineness to the creation of another concept, a master concept of "fact *qua* fact." If there is an ultimate fact, an undeniable fact, a terminal fact, then such a fact can serve as a "foundation" upon which one can base a theology, the Apostle's Creed, even a system of theology. So the issue is not whether the word *fact* has all kinds of meanings— it surely does and these can be ascertained quickly enough in all kinds of contexts.

We have alluded to several of the contexts already, wherein we contrast fact with law, opinion, art, interpretation, and so on. But the point we are making is that the notion of fact, as in "foundation in fact . . .," when used in theological contexts is, at best, a borrowed usage from historical and scientific contexts, and, at worst, an inflated and ill-begotten posit, trading on some intellectual conventions but quite without substance.

For the theological quest for the fact is richly invested with a meaning-content like this—that there must be some neutral and nontheological facts, which because they are facts, are also indisputable, definitive, religiously neutral, unanalyzable, and the warrant for, the cause of, as well as the correlative to the theological statements. The researches of many students nowadays, not least the Biblical and historical students, seem directed to isolating those minima, those *in re* elements, from which the theological statements can then be constructed. The theologians who want to ground theology must have nontheological facts; otherwise the very concept of fact, the inflated concept, is vitiated.

It does not do much to say that there are no such facts as yet discovered, for that makes the need look like one that can be satisfied by more empirical research. Actually, it is the ill-begotten general concept "fact" that misleads us to think that there is such a fact awaiting us. Some German historians and philosophers have thought about these matters over a period of many years. Dilthey, Mommsen, and others have said pertinent things, and lately R. G. Collingwood in England[7] and again numerous Germans have begun worrying afresh. For it became clear to some of them, just as it did to Wittgenstein, Waismann, and others on quite other grounds, that the general concept of fact was very odd.[8] So, from the theological quarter today, we get a rebuke of so-called positivist science, a criticism of past history and science that looked for the neutral and detached, the simple and unanalyzable "fact." The "positivists," who helped picture for others the world of atomic and discrete facts, waiting to be gathered up and interpreted—these thinkers, we learn, were completely wrong. Another and more adequate picture of facts is proposed, one which some recent German and American Biblical students insist will make "facts" so much the richer that a "new quest for the historical Jesus" will be possible.

Here the plot thickens, so we pause a bit. The search for the

---

[7] Collingwood's discussions in *The Idea of History* (Oxford, 1946) are extremely acute. He notes that the concept of "fact" is badly ordered to what historians finally find as facts. But he goes on to propose another inflated philosophical meaning.

[8] Note the account of Wittgenstein's reflections in G. E. Moore's essay, "Wittgenstein's Lectures in 1930–33," in *Philosophical Papers* (London, 1959), pp. 296 ff. These reflections can be matched and discussed by reference to Wittgenstein's later discussions, too.

foundations of theology via the facts seems to have foundered. Despite valiant attempts to find the foundations of theology in the facts about Jesus, nothing very conclusive ever appears to have been achieved. The pages of recent literature are strewn indeed with all kinds of researches, very refined and very detailed, but nothing that discloses a fact which could serve as a foundation, a guaranteed and indubitable starting point, something certain, simple, and also nontheological. In truth, these facts turn out not to be anything like this at all, for no science ever gets to that conclusive a point. There is no conclusive, determinate, and final description of anything, even Jesus of Nazareth. If one says Jesus is God, that may indeed be an ultimate statement, and one may want to say that "It is a fact that he is God"; but such a fact is not a discovery in the context of historical or any other kind of research, nor a fact in the context of a scholarly description, even the most complete imaginable. This is why the theological scholars have concluded so wistfully that the "kerygmatic Christ" is different from the "historical Christ," for it is as if nothing factual said in the latter context will lead one to saying something about Jesus Christ as God, Savior, Lord, or anything else that is religiously important.

But there is ingenuity afoot—some of it may even be deceiving. For some are inclined to say, not least those like Heinrich Ott and other systematicians, that the concept of fact has been too narrow and circumscribed. More than this, they urge that all kinds of other historical concepts, even that big one, "history," have to be refashioned. (This program—to sit down and voluntarily make up a new net of concepts—is something only very few people can contemplate.) If one does this, it is believed that "fact" will be seen to be part of a system of concepts, and that the whole system needs redoing. So, once there was "fact" in a positivist's system, and historians and researchers got nowhere religiously with that because the whole system in which it worked and had its role was wrong. Now it is proposed that a new concept of "fact" is needed—one that will see that "fact" can only be understood as a

systematic concept again, but within a different and more adequate system. What is called the "new quest" for the historical
Jesus will certainly increasingly call for tricky moves like this if it
is going to attract people who think that historical research has
much to do with theological foundations.

Once it indeed did seem that there were foundations in fact
for the tissue of Christian beliefs. Supernatural events, divine
interventions, miracles, God's purposes, and providence were
historical "facts" and intrinsically religious, open to a kind of
historical analysis. But J. B. Bury's harsh judgment is almost
typical of what is called positivism:

> Historians have for the most part desisted from invoking a naive
> conception of a "God in history" to explain historical movements. A
> historian may be a theist; but so far as his work is concerned, this
> particular belief is otiose. Otherwise indeed . . . history could not be a
> science; for with a "deus ex machina" who can be brought on the stage to
> solve difficulties, scientific treatment is a farce.[9]

Against this, one can easily enough understand that another
concept of fact might seem in order. And it has been proposed by
F. R. Tennant, R. G. Collingwood, Alan Richardson, H. R.
Niebuhr, and lately by several continental thinkers intent upon
making history less detached and more of an endeavor to get at
thoughts, at the inside of events, at the meanings—in short, at the
"lived" historical stuff. If historical concepts, especially "fact,"
can be stretched to include these, the "foundations" of theology
promise to be closer at hand. So, one can at least understand the
motives, if not these new concepts.

But an objection is in order. For the concept of "fact" is not
singular at all. There are indeed careful uses of "fact" in historical
disciplines, just as there are in the natural sciences. At one time,
people assumed that theological statements had their foundation
in historical facts. The quest became very earnest. But it turns out
that historical facts are just historical, and little else. They resolve

---

[9] J. B. Bury, *Selected Essays*, ed. H. Temperley, (London, 1911), p. 33.

historical doubts and play their roles primarily in an historian's context. So, too, with the scientific facts, be they what they may. The hard lesson to learn is that there is no transposition from one to the other. Theological statements, finally, if reducible at all, are reducible only to theological facts.

I V

I have no quarrel with research or with facts and their discovery. My concern is with an argument and with a concept of facts. For the difficulty lies in the conviction that there is a single and master concept of "fact" and correspondingly in the belief that there is a master state of affairs to which it refers. Indeed, a concept of fact has been widely popularized, often closely associated with positivists but also operative among historians, scientists, and even men of letters. This concept allows people to think that they know a fact when they see it and that facts are one guarantee we have, in theology as in other branches of learning, against subjectivity and prejudice.

The gist of this view is that the word *fact* means "fact" and that is all there is to it; that "fact" is systematically unmistakable, univocal, and plain; and that "fact" is determinate and definite, the same in all contexts. But this is wrong, for the meaning of "fact," the very concept, is not single at all—it varies with the intellectual context such that there is no one concept of fact; rather, there are many of them, and they do not overlap very significantly. Whether one operates with the general positivist conception or with a new and contrived one is not the point; the fault lies in assuming a master concept, positivistic if it be, or making one up, whatever the motives, skill, or scope. The legitimate alternative to the one concept is not another master concept but the acceptance of the variety of concepts which we can glean, if we are so inclined, and which are referred to by the same word *fact*. The only way to learn what these various concepts are is by not looking at respective factors, any more than one gets the concept color by looking at colors. One must, instead, learn how and what the word *fact* does in the many contexts we noted earlier (plus the several sciences), and not suppose a common meaning for the several uses or make a philosophical problem out of the situation where there is no common meaning.

Religious people are probably prone to thinking that if God is omniscient, then he must certainly have all the facts in hand. So, if one asks whether there are men on the other side of the planet Jupiter, some may say, "God only knows," as if God knows the facts about Jupiter, too. So, too, there must be facts, we are inclined to believe, that God knows about his son, Jesus, but that *we* do not know. Soon the picture of indisputable and elemental states of affairs, altogether independent of our schemes of learn-ing (history, theology, physics, and the rest), grows up to haunt us, to allure us, as the goal and hope of even our quest for the sacred. No wonder that facts are thought be to be sacred.[10]

But certainly this context of a God who "knows everything," to whom states of affairs and facts correspond perfectly, is neither a religious concept of God nor a meaningful one; and certainly it does little for the concept of fact. Anyway, it is very questionable whether most people need to know what God knows in order to become devout. The issue, though, is the concept of fact. Is this concept so primitive and plain that all other concepts must trade on it? Is it also true that facts are the simple elements out of which knowledge is constructed? On the contrary, there are no simple substantives called "facts," irreducible, plain, and atomic; nor is there any one concept of "fact" either. Instead, we have to note that "fact" always marks a distinction between what is *not* disputed "now," "here," "in this context," "under these circum-stances," "presently," and what *is* so disputed. Therefore, even within a kind of discourse—say, the study of the historical facts concerning Jesus—there is a moving line of demarcation between

---

[10] See J. R. Lucas, "On Not Worshipping Facts," *Philosophical Quarterly*, vol. 8 (April 1958), pp. 144–157.

what is and is not acceptable as "fact." This is not a fault of the research, nor is it a failure to keep one's concepts or one's meanings straight. The problem occurs because there is no big fact, final fact, discoverable by historical research, or, for that matter, by any kind of research into facts. The picture of the race getting closer and closer to the fact or facts, as if they were "there," waiting to be matched by thoughts and words, is a completely false one.[11]

Therefore, ever since historians and other research scholars have begun to look for religious "foundations" in the facts, skepticism has also grown. For with research in every field, the facts do not become plainer, as a superficial use of *fact* might suggest, but become more difficult to get at, more technical to state, and plainly upset the picture of "the realm of facts" with which one starts. So the facts about Jesus have become harder and harder to state, the more they have been thought to be a function of historical and critical studies. The line between fact and nonfact, the indisputable and the disputable, keeps moving the more skillful the researchers, the better the tools of the craft, and the wider the area of cultivation. How can one expect anything different? Anyone who tries to base his theology upon such facts finds them to be in flux.

"Fact" in all the empirical-like disciplines is not a determinable matter, because both the concept and the facts (that which is being described) are subject to a description that is never complete. We do not know what a complete description, even God's perfect knowledge, would be like, save such a description that would anticipate and settle every possible question. And we do not have that, not about Jesus or about anything else. We have no way to foreclose against the possible doubts except where the context

---

[11] Wittgenstein says: "But now it may come to look as if there were something like a final analysis of our focus of language, and so a 'single' completely resolved form of every expression" (*Philosophical Investigations*, I, no. 91, p. 43). See also Peter Herbst, "The Nature of Facts," *Essays in Conceptual Analysis*, ed. Anthony Flew (London, 1960), pp. 134–157.

or the texture of the discourse has already done that for us. "Every even number can be represented as the sum of two prime numbers" and "a heptagon cannot be constructed" are quite different from all those experiential statements that cannot be verified conclusively. For where an unlimited number of tests can be proposed and where the very terms are open and change in meaning as the inquiry progresses, there is no finality and no closure.

The thought of letting facts speak for themselves certainly makes sense in some contexts; and perhaps all of us can give instances when it makes a great deal of difference to say this. But to inflate this notion—as if for all possible contexts, including theology, there is a brute fact waiting to speak, unequivocally if we let it—is to make a new mythology. Is there a world of facts different from the world of words to describe them? Is there a bottom fact we finally come to, something really foundational? Or is there not? The convention is to say yes, as if facts existed independently and prior to language, waiting only for their proper expression. Then the facts must be the same through the ages, and only the theologies, the linguistic expressions, are different. Are there any such "same facts"?

An answering view, which we only noticed in passing earlier, says that "fact" is indeed not an independent and isolated factor. While I want to stress that there is indeed a work of man by which "facts" are constituted, this is not to say that facts are arbitrary, merely items in systems of thought, or a "function" (in the logician's sense of that word) of other beliefs. My point is a different one—namely, that there is the same fact and only different contexts in which we conceive it. Actually, we know nothing in the world to correspond to "fact" in this sense. What is a "fact" is so in this context or that. Usually what we call a fact is what we can reason from, what we can take for granted, what is agreed upon, and what (in this context, place, and for given purposes) we do not need to quarrel about and perhaps cannot. In this limited sense there are facts; but these are disputable the moment we learn how to raise questions that are relevant, and sometimes from different contexts. The overwhelming point to remember, which lays to rest the ghost of those peculiar philosophical longings that grip us ever and anon, is that there is no indisputable, no indubitable starting point—no fact—for any and all inquirers. We treat the word *fact* as if it were self-explanatory and ground-level, as if there were essential features of everything, open to inspection, falling under it.

And this is also the case in theology. It is simply a mistake to assume that empirical research and historical study will some day reveal "the fact," in virtue of which the foundation for theology will be laid once and for all.[12] The fault is again not in the researches, in methods, in subject matter, or in skills or lack thereof; it is, rather, in the very concept of fact, the inflated and fantastic concept, that promises to fit every kind of inquiry and ground the most strenuous and different endeavors, not least morals and religion.

There are facts to which eyewitnesses are privy. The maximum that an historical reconstruction of the time of Jesus can do is to tell us all the facts that contemporaries were then in a position to observe. The privileged access here is quite different from the access that a mathematician has to the mathematical facts; for here there is no privilege at all, though there is something we call the "expertise" and the training of the mathematician. But this is said only to remark upon the differences between "facts" in these two contexts; for the concept in the first instance is quite different from the concept in the second. It seems strange sometimes to have to admit that what is fact for the mathematicians seems like theory to an historian; and what is dubitable in one context may not be so in another, for even doubt is deeply hedged. The large point is, again, that there is no

---

[12] An example, now old but chosen because it is so typical, is R. Kittel's *The Scientific Study of the Old Testament*, trans. J. K. Hughes (London, 1910). The subtitle is revealing: "Its Principal Results, and Their Bearing upon Religious Instruction."

meaning of *fact* independent of all possible contexts and independent of all kinds of discourse; and therefore there is no way to assert a fact, religious or otherwise, that is a foundation against the doubts raised in the many different contexts of our daily life and learning.

So much for the concept of fact. If a man has doubts about religious matters, it behooves us to ask about the kind of doubt. Some doubts can be resolved by the appropriate facts; but facts are only indisputable and foundational to historical learning, to philological theory, or to this or that way of addressing the situations. There is no fact *qua* fact—all facts are historical, scientific, theological, etc., and are qualified and circumscribed by the kind of texture we use to discern them, think them, state them, and even look for them at all.

More importantly, there are kinds of doubts, too. There are some for which facts are irrelevant. Only a change in a mode of living will cause some doubts to cease. This is why the notions of a "brute fact" and the somewhat similar "basic law" have to be resorted to with such care. All kinds of things were once considered basic, inexplicable, and simply to be accepted, only later to be further explained. It is not an idle matter for some scientists to note that some kinds of learning can never assume that laws or facts are basic, for surely many processes of inquiry would have been stopped dead in their tracks long since if others had not asked questions and even speculated a bit. Anyone who thinks, therefore, that one can know a fact that is not a fact in a context and is anterior to all contexts—a fact, in other words, which is a kind of basic existent—is wrong. If there are any, we cannot know of them. Discovering "facts" like these is something like discovering uncaused events; if there are any, we can never be sure that their causes are not still undiscovered.

My interest in this chapter is not to disparage the intellectual life but only two mistaken ways of looking for foundations. I began by saying that the foundations of theology seemed to be wanting. It seems to me that in looking for "foundations," theologians are often misled by two words, *being* and *fact*, which because they work in certain familiar ways, here and there, both in everyday speech and in special disciplines too, soon are made into imposing and general concepts. One of the reasons that many theologians think philosophy is so important (to them and to their theologies) is that they believe philosophers "state," "express," "discover," "think," etc., the general and inescapable concepts all of the rest of us use and must use, only they do it better and with all the meanings, as it were, in-gathered. The concepts of "being" and "fact," when fleshed out and made inclusive of all the meanings of related words (*is, exists, in fact, as a matter of fact, the facts, to be*), are certainly a very rich brew. The contention has been here that when these concepts get so inflated, they no longer can be used to refer at all; and it is a mistake to be led by them to look for being *qua* being and for the ultimate fact.

V

Is this to say that there are no foundations? Is theology, as some are fond of saying, only a myth? For without foundations, what is to keep us from saying that theology is only rumor, opinion, a story, talk, signifying nothing? But a little caution is in order. Once science was talked about, too, as if it had to have foundations, discernible by these special philosophical talents and tools. Ethics has been so described; so, too, the arts, psychology, politics, and even diplomacy. Religion, and particularly theology within Christian and Jewish circles, is still so conceived. But certainly some mistakes are being made here.

There are indeed foundations. Sciences do have their facts, and so do historians, sociologists, and the rest. There are conceptual foundations also of a variety of kinds. But the lesson to learn from these is that the facts are not the same for all—there is no one fact—and the facts are not plain! The facts can often be seen at the end of the inquiry, not at the beginning. Once again we can note that the meaning of *fact* is not the same in all the disciplines, nor is there a common referent for that familiar expression. Facts are what is so in this context and that.

We must note, too, that Christian people have for a couple of thousand years attached great significance to the fact of *Consummatum est*. Something was settled and is therefore ready; some things have been done; sin and death are vanquished; God is in Christ, and Christ has been born, has lived, has died, and been raised from the dead. In a certain way of speaking, these together make the fact, the foundation, of at least Christain theology. It is not my point to defend this fact or these facts. But the logic of foundations is my task. This fact (putting these separable facts together as a single story) is, of course, not correlative to the inflated concept of fact that bewitches us when we ask, without qualifications, "Is it a fact?" On the other hand, is it not facile to say that Christians have a foundation in such a theological or religious fact?

Even though Jesus was an historical personage, however, historical facts are not the exclusive foundation for theological assertions, any more than biographical facts about men and animals are the foundation for the doctrine of the creation of all things. There are many difficulties here that must be ferreted out, but most of them are really conceptual rather than empirical. Also, it is hard to see what new historical facts or what new facts in any scientific context of inquiry could possibly do to the concept of fact that people use in the great creeds and other affirmations of faith.

These matters are, of course, greatly tangled today, not least because some theologians have wanted to give up facts altogether, letting the men of science and history have facts on their side, while the theologians have values or "meanings." But once that game is begun, even if it is played with "kerygmatic significance" (which is supposed to make Jesus Lord), then another arena has to be entered—that of the philosophical theologians of being. And another, detailed analysis is in order to show that theological facts are not simply meanings and that the old formula *adaequatio intellectus cum re* holds for theology as it must for other disciplines, too.

6

Language and Theology

There has been much talk in religious circles about the condition of theology. In one sense, remarked upon in other chapters in this volume, there is a kind of learned "theology" that relates to a living language of faith in about the same way that political theory in a university relates to the enthusiastic advocacy of political allegiances and convictions. Theology, if we mean that kind of historical study of religious ideas, need be no more religious than political science is political. Those who want to politicize everything, including the scientific study of politics, are under the delusion that there is no such thing as a nonpolitical study of politics. But there is. So, too, is there a nonreligious study of religion; and it would be downright silly not to acknowledge it. Whether it deserves all of its accolades is another matter. For reasons that may be analogous to politics, the detached study may seem both useless and an indulgence when other matters are at stake.

It is not "theology" in the above extended sense, however, that causes the misgivings with which I am here concerned. When people say that theology is dead, they do not suggest that the scientific study of religion is disappearing or is completely pointless. Rather, they seem to be talking about the language of faith,

An earlier version of this chapter appeared as "Language and Theology" in *Harvard Theological Review*, vol. 58 (1965). Copyright 1965 by the President and Fellows of Harvard College.

the kind of theology we find in creeds, in the Bible, in Calvin, in the mouths of Apostles, Puritans, Saints, the converted, and the persuaded. For a variety of reasons, many of them not very clear, it is charged that just such a language, such a theology, and such a way of talking about God are no longer viable. It is contended that believers and theologians have to seek a new idiom altogether.

It is furthermore contended that the meanings of that theology are probably all right. But the thesis is frequently projected that the linguistic medium by which we say those meanings is what has become trite and obsolete. We live in a time when the need is expressed over and over again for new translations of everything old. Thus we tend to reinforce the notion, by thinking about all of this, that this primitive and plain kind of theology must be retranslated, too, into a more modern linguistic garment. But words are one thing and concepts perhaps another. With the great enthusiasm today for a certain kind of linguistic study and continual retranslations on the part of students of the Bible, and with what looks like a strong and growing interest in linguistic philosophy, there are bound to be a few confusions generated. These pages are intended to head them off.

I I

Most natural languages, like French, German, and English, seem to be, and are to their users, relatively stable. Very few of us ever mark any great changes in the language that is native to us. Of course, the lexical stock grows a bit, but we are never very clear whether a word is new to the language or new to us; and it does not make much difference anyway if our aim is only to learn the word. Furthermore, we have been taught all kinds of rules of grammar, and these scarcely change. Almost everything new fits into the same grammatical context. Even if we have not been taught rules explicitly and clearly, as once was the case with educated people, we have certainly inferred them. The more we write and the more we talk, the more we conform to certain standards. If we do not, we use language to little purpose. And there is a kind of earthly wisdom, whatever else it might be to the philologist and the professional students of language, in getting rules clarified for ourselves and our heirs.

This stability of a core vocabulary and grammar is, of course, somewhat misleading. Because we trade on a vocabulary and on what seems like a manageable number of habits and words, we certainly also see to it that education goes on. Old teachers speak to young children and vice versa, and understanding goes on fairly easily and well. Therefore, our working language, the one that is our greatest tool for so many purposes, bridges the generations and usually without noticeable strain. In fact, changes in popular morality are more obvious, if the folklore about these matters can be believed, and more difficult for the older generation to comprehend, than differing patterns of speech. Despite these convictions about the perpetuity of language, however, it does change and very rapidly. One does not have to be a historian of language to discover changes. One needs only to stop the easy flow of language and think about it, not just with it.

Which of us has not read the language of the King James Bible and discovered to our surprise how different it is from present-day English? Of course, it may be the other way around. Maybe we have been taught our religion in King James's English and every other translation since seems less sonorous, rich, and deep. But either way, there are big differences. Shakespeare's plays, spoken in the manner of the Elizabethans, would certainly be unintelligible to most of us in this day. It is fortunate that the written language is still sufficiently recognizable to give us relatively quick access. But if we push back to Chaucer's texts, let alone the pronunciation of his day, we are in the presence of something almost as strange as a foreign tongue. Yet there are only a few more generations involved. In any case, most of the European languages have changed so drastically that the twentieth-century reader cannot understand the words of a person who antedates him or her by twenty generations.

These changes, however, are almost imperceptible as they occur. John Adams's mother must have believed that her son was learning the same fine English she had learned in her infancy. So, too, with most mothers since. Yet the language changed—often more rapidly than popular morals, though more slowly than much of learning (at least until relatively recently), quickly compared to biological traits, and sluggishly compared to political fortunes. Oddly, perhaps, the thought of Plato, Aristotle, the Old Testament, and the New has survived these losses and gains of language remarkably well; and this suggests, too, that some things, maybe moral convictions and beliefs, do not change as often and as radically as does the language. But my point here is only to stress that though it appears that language is a repetition of what one has been taught, this is not completely the case. The change is inexorable and also plain, once one is taught to perceive it.

Thus far, we can say with confidence that the major problems of understanding religious language do not arise because of this kind of change. Though the language may add new words while old ones die away, though sounds may vary greatly while the spellings by which we record them vary even more, still no particular difficulty arises at these junctures. Otto Jespersen tells us that the English language grew very remarkably when missionaries brought all kinds of Latin expressions into Old English. These were words appropriate to the Christian church and little else, such as *church, angel, devil, priest, mass, bishop*, and many others.[1] On the other hand, it is a well-known characteristic of language that those who introduce something foreign may also give the new phenomenon a native name. Thus the Germanic peoples, in contrast to those in the English speech-communities, did not so clearly add words as they did adapt those they already had. Thus, in adopting Christianity, they kept heathen religious terms for *god, heaven, hell*, and *devil*. And the pagan term *Easter*

---

[1] Otto Jespersen, *The Growth and Structure of the English Language* (Oxford, 1954), pp. 41 ff.

is used in English and German, whereas the Dutch and the Danes adopted the Hebrew-Greek-Latin term *pascha* (Danish *paaske*).[2]

My point is only to say that though languages change in vocabulary, grammar, and pronunciation, still people do manage to say the same things through the centuries. So the exact locus of the so-called problem that theologians today talk about so freely as the problem of a religious language does not arise because of these kinds of changes. When theologians speak of a vocabulary failing them, of their needing new ways to state meanings, this sounds like a radical remark about language; but in one sense of a "changing language," we can say confidently that all languages change in a variety of ways. Furthermore, these changes do not entail major losses or gains in our ability to say what we have to say. Or putting it the other way around, it seems that we can say the same things in modern English as we could in Old English, just as we can say things in French as well as German. Having something to say is still more of a problem than is the question of the availability of words. By saying this, however, I do not bind myself to the notion that having something to say means that one is a "mentalist," or that thought is a silent and wordless language. The point is rather, that with few words or many, old words or new, the chief requirement is to have something to say.

I I I

The theological issues, and probably some related philosophical questions today, are usually said to inhere in another kind of shift. It is alleged that many philosophical and religious words have either lost or changed their meanings. Because of this fact, it is contended over and over that communication is no longer

---

[2] These examples are taken from Leonard Bloomfield's chapter "Cultural Borrowing," in *Language* (London, 1935), esp. p. 455. In turn, the author gives numerous references for examples; cf. "Notes," p. 522. A related set of illustrations can be noted in C. S. Lewis's *Studies in Words*, 2nd edition (Cambridge, 1967), pp. 214–269, respecting the notion of "world."

possible. Perhaps this is to say, as a current mild and gentle
Protestant piety suggests, there is no longer any community. Thus
it is alleged that the language of the Christian church, its prayers,
creeds, Scriptures, and even formalized teachings are almost
unintelligible to men of the twentieth century because there are
no longer any shared meanings.

For a moment, we can let these charges rest. Their proportions
are what we are intent upon right now. For the allegation is that
the issue is not simply one language group versus another (for
example, early Latins versus English-speaking contemporaries);
nor is it either a question of users of Greek versus users of
German. Instead, we are told that "modern men," apparently
without regard for which language they speak, are simply unable
to comprehend the language of the church, again no matter what
its vernacular. If this allegation is at all sensible, the issues of
vocabulary, grammar, syntax, and phonetics, to which we referred earlier, are plainly not the most relevant matters for
consideration. Whether the vocabulary is old or new, the grammar the same or different, is seemingly irrelevant. The issue is the
meaning; and the meaning is apparently more like an idea than a
sound, a thought than a rule, and a concept than a physical thing.

Thus the pertinence of the plea for revising the theological
language. For it seems that language must "express" something;
and the notion of "expression" is so easy that it is positively trite to
most of us. Of course, language expresses thoughts and ideas,
mental acts and concepts; and it is in virtue of these that language
"means." To ask what a piece of language means is a sign of
earnestness; and to say that one does not know what some
language means is a sign that something is seriously wrong.

The diatribe against the language of the church today is
therefore extremely serious. I am not here thinking simply of
those clever philosophic fellows who say: "Metaphysics is meaningless; theology is metaphysics; therefore theology is meaningless." Nor am I particularly concerned here with people who
propose new criteria of meaning and then flail the ways of

speaking to separate grains of meaning from the chaff of the meaningless. These moves go on and have their special attractions and appropriate pitfalls. The charge about the language of the church, and from erstwhile sympathizers at that, is that the language of faith is simply pointless as it stands. Apparently its vocabulary is orderly and its grammar respectable; but be it in either the King's English or near-slang, almost as you wish, still it does not communicate because it does not mean anything. The meanings supposedly have to do with the differences between people then and now, but just *what* is hard to describe.

What does this charge mean? I submit that it does not have to do strictly with linguistic meanings at all. Therefore, it only sustains a confusion to ask for a revision of language, as if this were the seat of the difficulties. What is at stake is another network or scheme, not language, but actually another kind of convention or view. This is subtle and abstract, somewhat ambiguous, and perhaps also more a matter of pseudogrammatical and philosophical than literary doctrine. For the difficulties, if such there be, are described as if people hear the words but do not comprehend anything appropriate. Therefore, the welfare of religion in our day, not least Judaism and Christianity, is recounted as though literacy and readability, attending and hearkening to the words, are impossible in any deep and heartfelt way.

The difficulty in communicating with "modern man" (which is a highly regarded circumlocution in religious circles) lies not in the language but in the scheme of concepts that ordinary language is supposed to represent. The idiom for this issue is to the effect that words, and especially big religious words, are mere symbols. Supposedly, then, words, spoken or written, are deemed to be audible or visible representatives of something that is inaudible and invisible—namely, thoughts or ideas, or what we will call simply meanings. Because words "symbolize" something nonlinguistic, words also have meanings.

There is one glaring mistake in this, and it seems to have also permeated much of the current theological literature oriented to language as symbolic. For there is a defensible use of the word *symbol* to describe the formulating and standardizing of particular visible marks on paper to represent particular forms of speech. Therefore, writing a language is largely a matter of symbolizing a language. And one can assert rather blandly that the writing is not the language itself but a way of recording the language by visible signs. The upshot is then the symbol. But to go further by insisting that the spoken sound is also a symbol is a mistake. The sound is not on all fours with the marks on the paper. Of course, there is a sense in which one distinguishes between the sounds, too, and what one has to say. It would be absurd, admittedly, to have someone say that he was trying "to say" the sounds or the phonemes, when in fact he was using the sounds to say whatever he had to say. But the sounds are not symbols of the meanings in the way that marks on paper are symbols of words.

We need to be reminded of this by concrete examples. People use language in a wide variety of ways without writing it down, and it does not suffer any losses because of that. On the other hand, putting language into symbols, into marks on paper, has all kinds of advantages that one need not recount here. But the language can well be the same no matter what system of symbols one uses to record it. If one admits this much, then there seems little point to saying about a writing system anything more than that it extends the powers of language over time and distance. But language can be symbolized in a variety of ways. Does it follow from this that language itself is always and invariably symbolic? Here my point is simply that a very plausible dogma has taken over. That dogma causes us to think that meanings are kinds of events, objects, persons, or things lying behind language and for which language is supposed to stand. Then all of language, verbal and written, is a symbolic activity. But that is a piece of metaphysics, not a matter of common sense or scientific description.

Surely, it is not true that all speech is also symbolic. Sometimes the theologians seem to be saying just that. Then one has the anomaly on one's hands of arguing that whether spoken or written, language *qua* language is representative of something nonlinguistic, preferably what is called a thought, a meaning, or an idea. The point here is not to deny anything so obvious as the fact that language has meaning but only to ask whether we are sure that meaning always comes first, then speech and/or written words thereafter. We have already said that writing symbolizes the language, but does it follow that the spoken words are also symbolizations of thoughts?

The indubitable successes we have in translating from one language to another probably sustain our convictions. For if we say something in French, English, and German, we are strongly inclined to believe that the "something" is no one of these, that it is a nonlinguistic "something," only expressed in respective languages. Thus an inquiry into the language used seems almost trivial, especially if one is inclined to think that the propositions, concepts, or facts for which the words stand, be they French, English, or German, are the important matter. Thus words, whether spoken or written, seem to be substitutes for, expressions of, and vehicles respecting the nonphysical stuff that is being transferred or communicated with the words. Both popular beliefs and sophisticated reflection agree that words are not sufficient in themselves to account for the obvious and normal effects of speech among us. The powerful stimulation effected by language is deemed inadequate unless the words are symbols of the more spiritual stuff that seemingly guarantees, or even is, our meanings.

A kind of spiritualization of language takes place among us, and most of that finds its fruition in a notion that the realm of meaning is mentalistic, inside of our heads, and finally the sort of place or region to which a person has only his private and highly privileged access. For if we "mean" (now using that word as a verb) by some kind of intentional activity like thinking or knowing ("I know what I mean"), then there is no public and ruled access to anything but the sound and shape of the words. We can then see why Humpty Dumpty was so easily tempted to believe that words meant exactly and only what he wanted them to mean.

For words are indeed words, but meanings are not quite like them. We cannot see, hear, or apprehend the latter save by the same activity that makes them. Certainly, this kind of "mentalism" disguises many mistakes of a rather subtle sort. But there is also something very ordinary and popular about the view, and a lot of ordinary and feasible talk about symbols, thoughts, consciousness, and intending give it a currency among literate people.

I V

But our inquiry might best be served by seeing how we get into such a predicament in theology. One example may suffice. It is said that the word *God* has no meaning for modern men, that it is dead, irrelevant, and therefore quite pointless to repeat.[3] Though it is still in the active vocabulary of most people, and though very few people will ever use it in grammatically mistaken ways, still the meaning is said to be absent. Just what was the meaning it once had? It might well be said that people once talked about causes of everything and also the cause of everything considered together as the world, the universe, or even as creation. Now, the theme goes, there is no authority to talk so in the modern world. Therefore, *God* does not get any meaning any longer from scientific discourse or even from common ways of summing up things. If this be so, the concept "God" has almost disappeared. There is literally no thought-content being fed into the expression from much of anything. So, the thesis runs, the word *God* has no meaning. Once one meant "creator" or "maker," but now that cannot be meant.

A familiar dichotomy has come into play here—that between a word and a concept. The word, whether spoken or written, audible or visible, is taken to be a counterpart to the mentalistic

---

[3] This is the issue for Bishop Robinson in *Honest to God,* for Helmut Gollwitzer in *Die Existenz Gottes im Bekenntnis des Glaubens* (Munich, 1964), for Paul van Buren in *The Secular Meaning of the Gospel* (New York, 1963), and for numerous others since.

concepts. Unlike judgments or what more recent thinkers have called "propositions," which assert something to be the case, "concepts" typically refer and do not assert. In the rather long-standing lexicon of logic, "concepts" are taken to be the meaning-complexes by which we make our references to all sorts of things. "Judgments" and "propositions," utilizing concepts to be sure, were and are said to be our meaning-complexes, infinitely more complicated, by which we affirm or deny something to be so. These distinctions are rehearsed here not to teach them or even to reinforce them in any way, but only to give the lie to the difficulty the theologians claim to discern. For their argument seems to rest on this conventional bifurcation between physical word and mental concept, meaning and language.

Obviously, words do nothing much by themselves. They neither refer nor fail to refer. People do the referring, and most frequently with words. Likewise, concepts are meaning-complexes, but again, not by themselves. It is the organization of emotions, feelings, references, and a variety of thought-contents, which our behavior and its contexts require, that finally accrue into a concept. But a concept is, finally, a realized capacity, a power, accumulated in the life-history of an individual by which he or she does an enormous variety of things. Usually a concept is represented by a general term; and this has given rise to the mistaken view that a concept *is* a general term—this in contrast to a name. But it is what lies behind the general term or the phrase or even the sentence that matters. And the concept is that ruled ability with which an individual uses words—it is not again the words themselves—that matter. But other issues lurk here, too.

In passing, it must be noted that I do not intend to make light of the "concept/word" distinction, for it occurs very naturally and appropriately. But the particular problem is twofold: (1) whether the concepts ("meaning-complexes that refer") have to be conceived as though they are separate entities behind the ordinary speaking that goes on everywhere; this may be described in another way, which makes for the other aspect of the issue: (2)

whether there is a technical conceptual language, a language that is more meaningful, in which the concepts find their fullest expression. This view causes us to neglect the plain fact that conceptual meaning is really made by the way our ordinary language works. Therefore, there is no special arena of concepts, considered apart from words; for concepts are among the things that words express when they are used effectively and with regularity and in recognizable ways. Furthermore, there is no special conceptual language richer and better than ordinary ways of speaking. This does not say that there is no such thing as a study of concepts, but that language which describes concepts is not necessarily richer in conceptual meaning because it describes the way language works and means. Again the concepts are the abilities themselves.

If we revert to "God" for the moment, it is now widely reputed that language about God, whether in theology or the creeds, the Bible perhaps or even the liturgy, is said to be of little avail today because it does not mean anything. The theological sentences are no longer thought to be either true or false, worthy or unworthy, because no one can take as meaningful the propositions of which the sentences are said to be an expression. Why not? Because the concepts, the big meaning-complexes that refer, are supposedly dead. If we remember the duality already alluded to, then we have propositions being expressed in sentences and concepts being expressed in words (or combinations thereof). Without meaningful reference, theological and religious language has become largely vacuous.

Some such diatribe as this is leveled against much theology by some of the radical reformers today, as it was by Strauss and Feuerbach in the last century. Again we reiterate how serious this is; for this charge about concepts themselves makes the religious language supposedly only noise in the air or marks on paper. All of this has happened, too, because of continuing changes of a broad cultural and sociological sort, macroscopic modifications in ways of thinking and behaving denominated by such grandiose

terms as "the rise of science," "industrialization," "nonmythologi-
cal thinking," and the like. Whether there are still principalities
and powers may be a moot point, but now there are all these other
things. And the proposals to remedy these must be equally bold.
Obviously one cannot undo such social changes, but one can, if
some reforming theologians are to be believed, do something
about meanings.

Just what is not so clear, however. It is a little easier to
diagnose the illness than to heal it. But one way to address oneself
to such confounding issues is to try all over again to ascertain what
in the world was being symbolized. If we still have the religious
language around—and to a surprising extent it is, after hundreds
of years—we can do some kind of analysis, a type of theological
investigation into the meanings. Something like this goes on in the
pages of Paul Tillich, of Karl Rahner, of many interested in new
forms of ontology, along with some of the analysts, especially
those who do it at a distance. A supple penetration into concepts is
no easy matter, and whatever the skill is, and whatever one's
judgment about that skill, it is quite rare. But we do have all kinds
of proposals being made here. Some tell us that the word *God*
symbolizes "being" in general; others, the "ground-of-being," but
probably not an existing "Father-in-heaven," which is pure mythology and not a concept that refers at all. But maybe the words
being or *ground-of-being* do refer to something with which we all
have familiar access already. Some theologian-philosophers seem
to think that and are at great pains trying to show us how it is the
case.

For the moment, the issue is not the correctness of the new
concepts as much as it is the way of addressing the matter. Other
philosophically talented writers have identified *God* otherwise,
sometimes by analogy with familiar processes from which certain
unfamiliar abstractions can be derived, sometimes with subtle
inquiry into "necessity" and a host of other logical topics. Again
the issue before us is not this resolution or that, but the legitimacy
of conceiving the issue to make these and other efforts even

plausible. Apparently, the inquiry rests on a conviction that most of us do not suspect is at all arguable. Because, as a matter of course, we draw a distinction between words and their meanings, and because we hear and see words without knowing what they mean, we are also inclined to conclude that we think the meanings and that we speak the words. Therefore, we decide that the warrantability for the speaking rests on the warrantability of the net of the meanings—be they concepts or ideas, thoughts or notions. When the latter fail, then our speech becomes vacuous and trivial, words without thoughts signifying nothing.

Professor H. H. Price said years ago that there is a widespread need for "a unified conceptual scheme." He went on:

When the ordinary educated man speaks of "a philosophy," it is a conceptual scheme of this kind which he has in mind. Such a scheme, he thinks, will provide him with the wisdom which philosophers are traditionally supposed to supply. He needs, as it were, a map of the universe so far as our empirical information has disclosed it; and not a map of the physical world only, but one which makes room for all the known aspects of the universe, physical, spiritual, and whatever others there may be. He needs it nowadays more than ever, since for good reasons or bad the Christian metaphysical scheme has lost its hold over him. . . .[4]

Therefore, the task seems plain: all that is needed is another conceptual scheme lying behind, as it were, our ordinary words. Professor Price's ruminations are very guarded, but his view could certainly give promptings to the more extravagant views of many theologians. For the task of so many theologians today is spoken of as being "constructive" rather than simply "analytic" (just as Price and other philosophers agree that clarity is not enough); and by this is understood the sketching of a conceptual system that will bring vitality back into the words of preachers. For a variety of reasons, the Christian conceptual backdrop is now thought to be

---

[4]H. H. Price, "Clarity Is Not Enough," Presidential address to the Mind Association, July 1945. Reprinted in H. D. Lewis, ed., *Clarity Is Not Enough* (London, 1963), p. 38.

clearly shattered. On the one side, there is the history of criticism—both lower and higher—of the Scriptures. There is, too, the decay of metaphysical confidences; the rise of sciences has given new contexts for *sin, creation* and other big religious words. The upshot is that the conceptual backdrop, what Price called "the conceptual scheme," is not there anymore. Correlative to this is the fact that people do not believe in Christian teachings, but they still want to be ethical and religious. The diagnosis of the unbelief proposes that because of the decay of the former, therefore the latter; because of a tattered conceptual scheme, there is little or no belief among the educated.

But surely some criticisms are now in order. For one thing, it seems strange to say that unbelief is fundamentally caused by the breakdown in the conceptual scheme. One would certainly have to examine the cases as they arise and discuss the respective persons and their inabilities to believe on a case by case basis. Besides, the phenomenon of unbelief is as old as belief. Also, it seems that widespread and popular belief in religion is more like widespread political allegiance—a consequence of convenience, acquiescence, and indifference, as much as a result of meaningful discrimination and thoughtful decision. Just what religious unbelief is among the educated today is equally difficult to say. Exactly what the breakdown of concepts has to do with it is a very complicated matter.

But the other matter, the argument respecting theological language resting on this layer of concepts, is another kind of issue altogether. For here there is a dogma at work, a dogma very close to most intellectuals, about language and how it is constituted. It is so thoroughly embedded in our habits of thought and ways of talking that we think it is simply a matter of common sense. Because our language piles up—after a while and amid all its changes—certain speech-forms and meanings which maintain their identity, we are inclined to leap to the conclusion that there is a realm of meanings explaining these identities and regularities. Speech habits seem pedestrian and mean compared to mentalistic realms of spirit. And all the useful distinctions between words and meanings, thoughts and sounds, and ideas and marks on paper seem to feed our proclivity to a metaphysical view of language.

Thus, my inclination is to view the current theological desires for new theological and conceptual systems as largely a consequence of a mistaken view of language. In contrast to the mistaken view, there seems to me to be no single view of language even possible. There are, though, interesting accounts of the meanings of many words. But there is no single philosophy of language, no single explanation of how meanings are bestowed, for there is no conceptual scheme, behind words, that can be grasped by the special tools of abstract reflection, dialectic, or subtle inference. This does not deny that ordinary language or, for that matter, scientific language involves concepts, or that religious language also involves them; but our point is that the conceptual meaning is achieved and often even discerned within the science or the religion, not by an outsider, a philosopher, or even a theologian.

This being the case, it can be said that there is no special science, be it even philosophy or theology, that lays hold of these meanings in a primary and underived way. And the thought that somehow a kind of learning or a kind of declaring of a very abstract sort will do it is absolutely wrong. Of course, it is possible to describe the word *God*, and in principle this will mean not simply the marks on paper but also the meaning; for words studied without their meanings are as much an abstraction as meanings without words. Nonetheless, it is feasible to describe *faith* as well as faith, *God* as well as God. Anything said here has not denied a whit the possibility of describing even the concepts indigenous to religions. But it is one thing to argue and talk well with such concepts and quite another to talk *about* them. The issue here is that there is no special access to conceptual meanings via the talk about them. The reflection and language by which we describe them does not impart meaning to them. Unless they had that already, there is no particular point to worrying about them

and no reason to suppose that meaning is going to be given by
further description.

Considering this legitimate descriptive role of a kind of study
of language (even its concepts) gives one serious pause respecting
the pretentious promise of so many theological—and philosophical—writers who write as though they can confer meanings if
they are just inventive and comprehensive enough. To the contrary, there is no artificial and extraterritorial way of doing that.
Meanings are an intimate part of the situation in which language
is used, where speakers and writers talk in order to secure the
listeners' and readers' responses. Meanings have no other status
and location than that.

This brings us to what might be called the *positive suggestion*,
granted some kind of crisis in theological language.

V

There is no doubt whatsoever that language can be described,
for it is being done continually. Furthermore, it is pertinent to
remember that phonemes, marks on paper, letters, and words can
be distinguished from meanings. Just how meanings become
connected with linguistic forms is an interesting study in itself.
The point I wish to make here is that this is not an esoteric and
odd business at all, though it is many-sided and complex. Furthermore, most of us have firsthand acquaintance with the processes
by which it is done. The task of exhaustively describing the
acquisition of meaning for every form of language has not been
done; and in fact it is extremely difficult to see how in principle it
could ever be done. For the situations that cause people to speak
include everything that happens and anything you can see and
imagine. In order to have an exhaustive and detailed account of
the meanings for every form of speech, we would also need an
absolutely exhaustive and accurate account not only of everything
in the talkers' world but also of the speaker too, his whims, desires,
cares and so on.

Because we do not have anything like this, our knowledge looks fragmentary; and many students of meaning are inclined to despair of an empirical kind of study. However, this is no cause for leaping to a general philosophical theory by which we can declare matters in one fell swoop.

On the contrary, there are ways by which we make meaningful all kinds of language; and we can know the "ways" well enough. We give meanings to language not by thinking abstract correlatives but rather by putting the language to work as hard and as thoroughly as possible. This is the secret of building a vocabulary, as we probably learned to our dismay when we were young. Because so many words on our list were simply of no use whatsoever, except to impress others, it was easy to forget the definitions and eventually to forget the words altogether. Words, even scientific ones like the highly artificial and contrived latinized words used in elementary biology, come to life when the occasions for their service are multiple, in laboratories, in reading, and in discussions. So, too, with our words of religion. Most of them get their meanings only when their role is pronounced. If there is no role, they too drop away.

The point that the theologians are addressing has, therefore, several sides. For it is a question of which part of religious language is really so dead today. Is it the discourse of the metaphysical theologians? Is it the language of the hymn writer? Is it the language of the psalmist and other Biblical authors? If we are talking about certain kinds of elaborate metaphysical theology, I believe it is quite clear that much of this is very dead indeed. Having read in great and tiresome detail many Latin pages of Chemnitz and an English version thereof, I feel particular enthusiasm in concurring. This is only to say, of course, that most of the metaphysical concepts, both of remote metaphysicians as well as the recent, have a jading effect upon us and do not strike us as being particularly illuminating or even as very relevant to our current inquiries. This is not to say that metaphysics as an inquiry is necessarily absurd—only that some metaphysical proposals are not very compelling. But the theme we are striking is that this ought not to obtain if what is believed about metaphysics is correct. For the metaphysically oriented theologians have said that the metaphysical concepts are actually more compelling and meaningful, more the essence and heart of the matter, than the language of hymns, sermons, and Scripture.

But we can agree that the metaphysical schemes are now widely deemed to be rather void. Because metaphysics has pretended to lay hold by a kind of conceptual cogitation in its purest and least sullied form, it has been held that metaphysics, and theology too, discloses the meaning of Scripture, hymns, and the rest of the religious language. We are back to an earlier point, where we tried to delineate the argument that says we need another theology in order to give meaning to our language, if not also to the other activities of religious organizations. If we are right, then the kinds of metaphysics familiar to us as the major systematic outlooks are simply not being actively espoused any longer. And if the diagnosis is correct, then the religious language of the churches is simply without its meaning or warrants for its meaning.

Of course, this is to suppose that metaphysics somehow bestows meaning on more ordinary expression. But this is certainly an outright mistake. Linguists have long since told us another story about how words acquire meanings. Descriptive linguistic studies about these matters are very detailed; and even an amateur's perusal of Mencken's *The American Language*, Jespersen's several works, Bloomfield's *Language*, and the now old work, *Words and Their Ways in English Speech* by Greenough and Kittredge, are enough to give us a feeling for the variety of ways that meanings accrue to speech. Suffice it to say that anything at all which adds to the working and viability of speech, be it behavior, gesture, circumstances, responses, references, or all kinds of accompaniments, also makes language meaningful. One of the ways we mark the meaningfulness of language is to see its long-term and pervasive effects. Even language that does not draw any prompt response may still affect the dispositions of hearers for subsequent responses.

Theology tells us, among other things, something about God and the world. It proposes beliefs, along with behavior and a certain refinement and intensification of the human response. However implausible the thesis may be, theology has been considered lately almost as a kind of semantics of religion, a kind of study of meaning. If one neglects words and their uses (what linguists call the speech-forms) and studies meanings in the abstract, one is really making semantics the general study of the universe. Something like that obtains with those theologians who are doing the modern theologies-of-meaning. This finally seems to be the appeal, too, of those who insist that metaphysical theories are the ultimate court of meaning.

I am contending, instead, that attention be paid to the actual workings of the speech-forms. When these are put to work in their appropriate contexts, then the meanings simply occur. Therefore, it is a mistake to treat metaphysics and theology as though they actually supplied meanings to more ordinary religious discourse. For if we are despoiled of metaphysical schemes, even grand theological schemes, it may be that this is a symptom and not a cause. Meanings belong to words when uses for them are at hand. The task for theologians, then, if they decry the vacuousness of religious language in the pulpit and the pew, is not to sketch a theory that will impart meaning as much as it is to suggest the "learning how" and all that that involves in the religious life. For the use of religious language, even the Bible and the hymns, liturgy, and prayers, is part of the business of learning to be religious. This is part of the "how" of being religious.

Once such uses are gained, words are no longer deprived of their meanings. It might be the case that much of the language of the churches is simply now a coarse kind of custom, quite without justification and point. Also it may be true that certain generalities about it of a sociological sort are justified—namely, that it is trite, defunct, and finally meaningless. But such generalizations do little to suggest the remedy, if that is what one seeks. There are all kinds of people who have mastered the use of religious language because they have also learned to be contrite, forgiving, long-suffering, and many more things. It is in that "how," that kind of learning, that religious language also begins to acquire a function and role.

I noted in passing that the decay of theology may be a symptom, not a cause, and to that issue I return once more. For the way that concepts are finally achieved, even concepts like "God," "sin," "grace," "salvation" and many more, is also by a kind of interaction between human responses and language. And this supposes a religious context of worship, faith, and concern. Indeed, there are concepts by which people refer to God and a host of other things in profoundly religious ways, but these concepts are achievements constituted in the long pull of educating the human spirit as to what religion is. If the concepts no longer have any life in them, if they mean nothing, then it must be that all the rest that goes into giving people confidence and faith that there is a God has also disappeared.

This is to say that there is no short road to restoring meanings. This is why the contemporary plea for a new theological scheme is so lamentable: it suggests that an artificial linguistic context, abstract at that, is really the best matrix for the very important words of faith to come to life; whereas the fact of the matter is that ordinary life—everyday existence—is that matrix. The knack is to learn how to handle oneself and the whole world. When that is being learned, certain words, Biblical words, come into their own. They become the tools of refining and intensifying one's daily life, and they become increasingly meaningful as one lives with and by them.

If religious words come to their meanings in this way, there is of course something for a theologian to study. Then he would not need to speculate and to invent meanings. He would have quite enough to help keep the concepts straight and their location in the intellectual economy as exact as possible. Then his task would be a kind of description of what is already achieved rather than an attempt to provide what is missing.

Perhaps it is also clear that the contemporary enthusiam for linguistic analysis on the part of theologians is another vanity if it is believed that this way of doing philosophy is the newest access to meanings. For the point of linguistic analysis is not to supply the missing meanings by the study of usages, whether on one's own part or the part of others. Therefore, the recent shift in philosophical emphasis is not the better way, analytic instead of speculative, to do the same thing. In fact, Wittgenstein's reflections on these matters are more in the direction of liquidating philosophy as the science of meanings than of inventing one more permutation of methods to provide them.

It may seem that all technical theological rubrics are hereby made taboo. But this is not the point. The argument with which we have contended says that the technical and abstract rendering of a pure conceptual language makes clear the meaning of the more ordinary and nontechnical kinds of speech that are widely used in liturgies, hymns, and Scripture. Or it is even said that the latter kinds of language contain in some involved way that which the technical language makes explicit. In any case, the technical theological language is said to make clear the meanings of the other kinds. But I have been arguing to the contrary. For the conceptual basis, even the achievement of the rich meanings which chart and state the Christian truths, is actually that more ordinary kind of speech, the language of fishermen, tax collectors, and tentmakers, rather than the more abstract variety. Therefore, the abstract language (technical theology, if you will) is now irrelevant and probably has lost its connection with this conceptual ground; and the way to make it significant and appropriate once again is to return to that primitive way of speaking. One might discover thereby that whatever meanings there are in technical theological discourse of a highly abstract and detached sort are a function of the ordinary language of ordinary believers and not the other way around.

One more illustration might suffice. The words *God* and *sin* and others, distinctive to religious people, have definite meanings. Such words have acquired their meanings over a long history. Words were connected with what was being said and done. They also changed what was being said and done. *God* and *sin* were used to refer to something in virtue of the roles they played in discourse. But it is also true that today many people enter the texture of such discourse, in our churches and our common life, without being aware of what is involved. Almost without number, people use these words wrongly or they use them to no point at all. This is because most of them do not know the concepts "God" or "sin" at all. Is this what the critics of supernaturalisms and the older theologies are saying? Maybe so. But there is a small difference that is the point of these remarks. A concept is learned by mastering the way the word is used—the tissue of reaction, stimuli, and responses. The long-term consensus within which the word has its place is a concept, and therefore the concept is more like a rule than a thing, a regular practice than an exceptional object, an exercise in *concreto* than an essay in *abstracto*. The theologian's task is primarily to isolate and articulate these concepts. To lose the meaning of the religious words is not like losing their definitions—it is more like losing the practice with which they were associated. To know the meaning of a word supposes keeping with the rule. And concepts are no good—they become just noises or just marks on paper when they lost the context in which they can be seen to be the rule. Rules are only rules if they are kept.[5]

Thus, theologians are in no position to justify the processes by which words have acquired their meanings. For justification is entirely out of order here. However sounds have been used in a multitude of circumstances, whether they are French, Greek, English, or Latin sounds, the fact is that meanings have been

---

[5] I am indebted for several suggestions here to R. Rhees, "Can There Be a Private Language?" in *Proceedings of the Aristotelian Society*, suppl. vol. 28 (1954), pp. 77–94.

ascribed. These circumstances of social and religious life were not invented, and neither were the meanings that grew with them. If religious words made great differences, they were also very meaningful. But all that was said with those meaningful words is another matter altogether. Religious men thought they were speaking truly about a world that was created and a God who died for the sake of the world. These beliefs indeed suppose religious concepts; for they make statements that tell us what is the case, and therefore they must refer. But it is one thing to see that language, even religious language, has meaning; it is another thing to see that it is true. A point to remember is that without the concepts no one could speak at all—for every language must be there before one can say anything. We all speak a language that is spoken; and it is only within that language that our words have their meaning.[6]

I have tentatively admitted the charge of the contemporary students of theology who insist that the old words do not mean anything to most persons anymore. But words do not "mean" all by themselves. They are not like some coins that have value because they are made of silver or gold, while also serving as media of exchange. Words may have meaning for one man and not for another. The question is the way they are used, how the person lives, and what applications the expressions are given. It is not the words that are at fault, as much as the persons speaking them. Therefore, the religious words are vain when nothing

---

[6] It must also be remarked here that religious language can also be sheer cant. There is a great deal of religious language that has nothing to go with it but the idiosyncratic uses of a small group or of influential individuals. Thus, one might make up rules and use words and ideas to accord with them. This is the way metaphysical systems frequently get their appeal, for they do no other work but what the author decides to let them do. Certainly there are esoteric religious groups and odd permutations on religious themes that are perpetrated in both practices and in theological treatises. But this entails another kind of theological criticism and demands a careful consideration of the religious authority of Scripture and how certain kinds of criteria are to be articulated and brought to bear upon the issues.

follows their usage, when the individual does not seem to know anything about the matters to which they refer and the way of life in which they were born. Then we can say sadly that people do not know what they are saying. To teach them that is one of the theologian's tasks.

7

Theology and Concepts

It is tempting to believe that Christianity is chiefly a religion of experience. There have been countless advocates of anti-intellectualist views of Christianity through the centuries. Usually these views have come in response to a stress on the role of doctrines, particularly the notion that belief in doctrines is the chief requirement of piety. On the positive side, the anti-intellectualists put a needful stress upon experience. Though the concept of "experience" is vague, it has had a marked vogue in both philosophical and religious circles. Varieties of religion have seemed to some thinkers to be varieties of experience, not varieties of theology. Philosophers have often said that "experience" is a datum, out of which come our concepts and even our beliefs.

But my task here is not to vindicate the concept of "experience." Perhaps we can all understand John Wesley's remark that faith is not a matter of "cold rational assent"; instead it is, he said, a disposition of the heart. However, Wesley did not disparage doctrines and the theological teachings when he said that, nor was he espousing experience at the expense of thinking. He thought the doctrines required a new quality of heart.

The concern for "experience" is also created by the dismaying prospect of having to decide which theology is the true one. In a quixotic sense, one difficulty today is not *no* theology as much as it is *too many* theologies. Theologies are rather freely and easily invented. We have a plethora of them—so many in fact, that it becomes almost a taxonomic science just to classify them and relate them one to the other. Part of that plentitude stems from the notion that "meaning" is their subject matter and that one must keep inventing and contriving theologies, if for no other reason than just to get the maximum meaning stated. In any case, theologies are now often like the speculative metaphysical systems used to be—they are schoolish, often idiosyncratic, and done in a variety of modes.

The peculiar problems engendered by the plural theologies will be discussed at considerable length later, in another context. Here I only remark upon the fact that the several theologies make the decision about which one to believe almost impossible. Certainly, one of the appeals made by "experiential" talk about Christian things is that it relieves one of the responsibility of having to decide between what seems undecidable. The talk about a Christianity without theology or doctrines takes two obvious forms. On the one side, there is the outlook that proposes that ethics is the heart of the matter. Then the Scriptures and the teachings are valued for their imperatives, not their indicatives. On the other side, there is enthusiasm for religious feelings and emotion, for an overpowering immediacy. Then the culmination of the religious life is said to be in Pentecostal experiences and a flow of pathos that is heartfelt and joyous.

Many issues would have to be considered in great detail to do justice to all the matters I have touched upon here. But one thing must be tellingly plain: that the Christian's life is a living synthesis of will, thought, and pathos, all three. Because sometimes an elaborate stress upon teachings tends to augment the cognitive, often at the expense of the volitional, the ethical, and the affectional, there is understandably a counter stress upon the latter at the expense of the former. Theologians and church leaders seem to be quite unable to keep an equilibrium in respect to all of these factors. In fact, the more educated one is, the more suspicion one has of the affective side altogether. Therefore, the emotional and the volitional tend to come back in rather bizarre forms, usually without the intellective teaching component at all. Religious worship, even the sermon, becomes almost like a many-sided stimulus, rather than something dialectical and intrinsically thoughtful.

Here it will be assumed that the teachings of the Christian faith are essential and formative of a language of faith. But as I argued elsewhere, that language, that first-person theology, is not merely expressive. If it is pertinent, intellectually legible, and in accord with the standards of orthodoxy, then it includes a host of concepts. Christianity is distinctively conceptual. Whether those concepts are used for cognitive purposes is another and difficult matter. We can surely recognize that some of theology aims to say what is the case, but my interest here is in the variety of religious purposes served by those concepts. Theology is not merely an ideology that with strident tones galvanizes the persons who entertain it. Instead, it proposes and requires a variety of thoughtful uses. It supposes consideration and a gradual assimilation.

In subsequent pages, I will discuss a variety of aspects of that conceptual and dialectical richness that Christianity proposes. Much of what I say here could be typified as remarks bearing out Kierkegaard's thesis that the Christian teachings project both dialectical and conceptual differences, on the one side, and equally differentiated qualities of pathos and subjectivity, on the other.

I I

Theology as the language *of* the faith, and not *about* it, is not a medley of personalized and ruleless jottings. Instead, it is a tissue of names and concepts, propositions and views, about God, about the world, and about a host of familiar human conditions. My purpose in these pages is to look at what concepts are and do within theology.

An aquaintance once asked me to identify what it was that a U.S. Government official had been talking so volubly about with a group of American Indians. The troublesome matter turned out to be the concept of "economic exploitation of natural resources." My interlocutor, a major figure in the Indian community, confessed to not knowing what that meant. It was not easy to say; for any definition in circumstances like that will have certain obvious inadequacies. Furthermore, to understand a complex concept like that is not simply to have words at one's command, nor is it to have a definition or a group of synonyms at one's disposal.

The concept noted is, indeed, a meaning-complex. After much discussion and use, the notion of an "economic exploitation" (rather than other kinds of exploitation) and the notion of "natural resources" (rather than other kinds of resources) have become operative in the literature and discourse of a relatively large number of people. Seen formally, and admittedly seeing here only the most schematic similarities, concepts are meaning-complexes by which we refer but do not assert. So concepts like "man," "animal," and "thing," as well as "God," "grace," and "economic exploitation of natural resources," are minimally the means by which we refer. When we assert something about something (what logicians call "stating a proposition" or plainly saying something), then we must use concepts. Concepts empower our asserting, for they give us something to talk about. But this is not all that concepts are, obviously enough!

Admittedly, the technical expression *concept* puts a rather formidable cast over something with which we are already familiar. It is well, right here, to note that many people become competent at using concepts without even knowing that they are using them. For example, when I say that "the trees are lovely," I am thinking about trees in general and no particular tree at all. The learning by which I come to use a general word like *trees* is very interesting and quite different from the way we learned to use *tree* in the first place. Our language is much richer in concepts than it is in names; and most of us learn the concepts in a variety of ways that defy assimilation to any single pattern.

Concepts are not simply words. Quite properly, we distinguish between words and their meanings. Often we are tempted to think that words are physical noises or marks and that meanings are spiritual and mental, somehow only refracted and expressed by the words. What we are saying about words and meanings does not speak to this latter point at all. I wish to separate the physical marks and noises, the words, from the meaning-complex. What, then, is the meaning-complex? It is altogether too easy to assume that it must be something refined and nonphysical. Here I propose a different way of thinking about the matter. When one understands "economic exploitation of natural resources," the criterion for that understanding is what one can do with that concept. To understand a concept is not simply to be able to define it but to be able to do the proper things with it. So, with the above, one judges the rapacious activities of the oil barons and the lumbermen who cut down forests without ever replacing the trees or counseling conservation. One does something in virtue of a concept—namely, judge, evaluate, compare, distinguish, describe, consider, pretend, etc. The very complicated array of ways in which "economic exploitation of natural resources" becomes an ingredient in all kinds of discourse among historians, moralists, politicians, economists, as well as innocent bystanders, is the meaning-complex. After a while, one knows that there are right ways to use this concept and wrong ways, too. But that is not another kind of conceptual knowledge. Instead, it is a function of what we call the understanding of a concept.

Concepts are not spiritual entities, nor are they simply "things." They are not meanings either, if we mean by *meanings* some kind of evanescent halo clinging to a word or phrase. They are more like personal powers, like potencies, like skills and abilities, than they are like things. But they are not occasional and accidental, either. *To have a concept* is a deceptive expression because it leads us to look upon concepts as things to be possessed. Clearly, a concept is not an acquisition like that at all. One does not "have" it even in the way one has a definition or the way one has a word when one is learning a language. Sometimes we have students recite a word-list in order to enlarge their vocabularies. But a word is not so limited and poor a thing that reciting it, mouthing it as it appears in a list, is really enough. One must also learn to say things, on one's own, with a word. Knowing a language is not quite the same as remembering and reciting a word-list. So, too, with concepts, though there are differences between words and concepts that begin to come into view. One "acquires" concepts, but not usually by reciting, memorizing, and getting words into one's vocabulary.

Concepts are acquired, but in a way that a capacity is realized, not as things are acquired. They are learned, but usually not directly. One gets a concept firmly when he masters the appropriate ways to refer, to judge, and to describe. And these actions are not highly standard. They are as varied as one can imagine. Most concepts are "enabling"; and one learns a concept by getting in on some aspects of what it enables one to do. The richer the concept, the greater the enabling. Some concepts—e.g., that of the "round world"—mean so much because they enable one almost indefinitely. No limit can be drawn around the number of things that are sayable and thinkable with that concept. This is part of what is meant by saying that such a concept is open-textured, though this does not mean that it is ambiguous or vague. Instead, it is to say that the concept is very powerful and hence exceedingly meaningful.

Concepts are both the consequences of a wide range of activities and progenitors of them. Concepts, Wittgenstein notes, "lead us to make investigations; are the expressions of our interests, and direct our interests."[1] Again, we learn concepts in an incredibly rich variety of ways, too. Concepts are like tools and instruments, not least of our language, but also and often of our purposes, interests, loves, morals, curiosity, and even our religious faith. So the number of ways in which we measure teaches us

---

[1] Ludwig Wittgenstein, *Philosophical Investigations*, No. 570. He also says in *Foundations of Mathematics*, trans. G. E. M. Anscombe (Oxford, 1956), p. 194: "And concepts help us to comprehend things."

about the concepts of "inches," "yards," "meters," "miles," and "furlongs." It makes all kinds of difference which concepts one uses. Again, it is the competencies, the abilities, the enabling for a variety of tasks, that is the complex we call a concept. We do not read concepts from a printed page—we ordinarily acquire them as we would a skill or a technique. To have a concept is not to have only a word; rather, it is to have a way of speaking, doing, judging, evaluating, etc. Wittgenstein, again, noted that a concept could be compared with a style of painting. While admitting that neither styles of painting nor concepts are arbitrary, Wittgenstein called attention to the fact that there were differing concepts, schemes of them, but that these differences did not mitigate in the least the ability to use concepts to describe facts of nature.

I I I

An obvious feature of a person who has understood concepts in a given field is the strengthening of his or her ability to talk and to write. Certainly, talking and writing often illustrate a use of concepts. This is the case with religious concepts, too. From within the histories and literatures of Jews and Christians, plus religious practices, all of us have learned a large number of concepts. The Christian concept of *agape*, or love, is a typically familiar one. But there are more—God, hope, grace, repentance, sin, guilt, sanctification, holiness, faith, creation, Savior, Lord, crucifixion, gospel, forgiveness, and many others. Many of these words are otherwise familiar; but it does seem that in specifically Jewish and Christian contexts, one does something distinctive with them. This distinctive power is tied up very concretely with the expectations and qualities of being a Jew and/or a Christian, with attendant forms of life, of concern, and of emotion. But still, one can learn from them also how to talk very effectively and comprehensively. One can pray with them, sing, confess, praise God and his creation, describe, judge, and, of course, simply make theological remarks.

For theology is (considered by itself, not thinking of its effects for the moment) a linguistic use of religious concepts.

In many intellectual pursuits, the only employment of the concepts that is even plausible is a linguistic one. Addison said that Milton's poetry, especially *Paradise Lost,* "has by the nature of its subject, the advantage above all others, that it is universally and perpetually interesting. All mankind will, through all ages, bear the same relation to Adam and Eve, and must partake of that good and evil which extend to themselves." If one wishes to speak nobly about the power of language, even theological language, this is certainly testimony to what its concepts can do. For poetry, as well as prose, uses concepts; and the power that great poetry yields is often due to the skillful blend of imagery, concepts, figures of speech, and metaphors.

But concepts do other things besides empowering one to speak and write. We are indebted to concepts for changed dispositions, for creating and sustaining emotions, for enlarging sympathy, for stimulating passion, and even for creating the virtues. Our stress, however, is not simply upon the many things that language can do for us, but rather upon the fact that concepts empower all kinds of nonlinguistic phenomena, too. These meaning-complexes, various as they are, also are exercised in our lives in nonlinguistic ways. Thus, it is a little strange to have the concept of holiness only producing more talk about holiness and maybe generalities about the problems of personal living. The concept of holiness also has the power of converting a person from unholiness to holiness. If the concept does not begin to do that, we have good reason for saying that one has misunderstood it. A customary and even cursory way to exert oneself with a concept is plainly to talk with it. But concepts also make it possible for one to do something in addition to talking and writing. The words found in theology level peculiar requirements against those who hear them. Understanding them is not a matter of only using more words. Wittgenstein noted this when he said: "How words are understood is not told by

words alone."[2] In religious societies it is often important to be
reminded that the very meaning of a word like *holiness* is grasped
and exerted not by discourse alone but by a new quality and form
of life. Thus it is important to remember that what we are saying
about concepts does not suggest that concepts are initially spiritual
and mental and that they subsequently get translated into either
speech or deeds. The linguistic employment is not a translation at
all. For concepts are not present to the mind in a nonlinguistic
way first and then only exemplified and deployed in verbal
fashion afterwards. Here the orientation is wrong. The point is,
rather, that concepts have as part of their meaning, part of the
complex, this power to be extended in speech. So, too, they have
as part of their very meaning the empowering of nonlinguistic
and behavioral changes. In fact, they are not understood unless
such changes are effected.

One aspect of theology is simply a highly technical and even
abstract description of religious concepts. Much of what goes on in
academic circles under the rubric of "theology," about which
people complain because it is impractical, is simply the description and study of the religious concepts. These have become
entangled with systems of concepts stemming from science, politics, and other endeavors. The task of disentangling and making
clear these religious concepts is not a case of using them. It is one
thing to use the concepts and quite another thing to teach
theology in such a way that the upshot is the actual employment
of these concepts by the pupil. Our major point could be made
this way: that one consequent, not altogether unlikely or inappropriate, would be that some persons might learn to do theology
themselves. Another and more significant use of the concepts
would be to help constitute a religious life. For there is a way that
one comes to believe so that a religious form of life ensues.

---

[2] Ludwig Wittgenstein, *Zettel*, No. 144 (Oxford, 1967). Further along in that
book (No. 387) we find Wittgenstein saying: "I want to say: An education quite
different from one's own might also be the foundation for quite different
concepts."

Indeed, the religious concepts occasion believing in such a way that one can talk with and about one's beliefs, but they also authorize all kinds of dispositions, feelings, passions, virtues, and deeds that make one's daily living something distinctive. They even produce another view of the world and human life. Religious teachers might want to insist that religion itself is a kind of education, quite different from what one would otherwise acquire. Our Lord taught men to live in such a distinctive way that Christian concepts have their foundation in that kind of education. But one can move the other way, too, from the concepts to the life. The New Testament does the former, while we do the latter from the New Testament and other literature.

Another way to say these things is that concepts are those particular ruled functions in our lives that we can characterize and give names to. All of us know the concept "pain"; for it has a very peculiar and patent utility for all of us. We have no substitutes for it, but we do have a large number of words by which to describe pains. The concept "pain" has all kinds of functions. We call a pain something that has a discernible connection with other experiences, that has only such and such qualities, and that occurs in surroundings that are fairly normal. We can expatiate freely about pains, describe our own and others' pains, and call attention to our needs thereby. I can be motivated to take another to the doctor because of his pain (and his apt use of the concept "pain"); I can be motivated to reduce the pain in the world and thereby acquire a new conception of my life. Animals, who have no range of competencies like that which goes with "pain," cannot decide to change the world. Thus we can say about the concepts proposed by the religious literature that they are discoursed about at length in theological treatises, that hopefully they permit their users to talk and think about God and the world, but also that they can be employed to refashion one's life and even to remake the world.

But a further differentiation of Christian concepts is in order, for there are many strange things about theology. Most of these are overlooked if one always likens theology to familiar batches of knowledge or if one is too struck by the notion that theology is, after all, knowledge of God. So we have to remember that theological teachings have also the power to commission their hearers. To be commissioned is to be given something to do. Religious teaching challenges people out of their complacency into a radical kind of behavior It makes disciples of the hearers. Therefore, to understand theology and to evince a command of its concepts is to be spurred, to be humiliated, to be stirred to contrition, to be prepared for joy. There is even a way to understand all human beings as if they were profoundly sick. This is also a Christian way. The Christian mode of talking is supposed to completely alter the way of sick lives, and the task is to cure one person at a time. Again, such a strenuously different use for teachings is easy to lose when we are so quickly seduced by analogies. Nowhere does one find the New Testament, for example, suggesting that this remedy can be used for a large group or a whole society. Rather, the New Testament always keeps one-at-a-time before the reader. It is individuals who are converted, even while nations are indeed being addressed. The political focus of Christian concepts is something altogether new and, on the face of it, quite questionable. But more of that subsequently.

IV

I propose here to note some of the distinctive features of Christian concepts, differentiating them from a large group of others. There are, for example, concepts which grow up in specialist contexts. These are indigenous to a craft or discipline, and only those who practice the craft or discipline share the concepts. Most of the concepts of scientific fields are like that. Physics, mathematics, genetics, and much of modern linguistics, for example, provide a motley of concepts, which one can get inside of only by becoming a specialist oneself. Within the broad spectrum of theological studies there are specialist fields, too. So, for example, the technical studies of ancient literature, including certain kinds of concern with the Bible, have produced a technical vocabulary and technical concepts. Most of the time, however, it is clear that such scholarship upon the Bible is prosecuted with a different set of concepts than is the religious life described within the Bible. And that is quite all right. The historians' finely developed techniques for describing the history of Israel are carried on in a different group of technical concepts than the historical careers of the Jews in ancient Israel were articulated by. Obviously, there might be an overlap of usage here, and that would arise naturally enough when an historian or Biblical scholar tried to adequately describe his subject matter. The histories about peoples must also take cognizance of their conceptual schemes.

So, too, the Christian scholars who describe the New Testament and the thought of its authors often use conceptual schemes that are quite different from those with which the primary authors were familiar. It is a commonplace now in academic circles to note that the description of a Communist's conceptual scheme is not itself a part of Communism. The descriptive concepts are not Communistic, even though Communist concepts are described. So, too, with that part of academic Christian theological studies that is descriptive. Much of it utilizes concepts that are so general that they can be said to be those of "literary critics" or "historians" or "textual critics," whose concepts stay the same whether they study lyrical Greeks like Homer or ardent Jews like Samuel or vivacious Christians like Paul—each of whom employed quite different concepts from the others. One point to be made from this is simply that a certain kind of academic study has been perfected in which the conceptual scheme employed has a kind of neutrality quite unlike that of the concepts and lives therein studied. The point being made here, then, also allows one to see how various specialist concepts actually are. They are often artificial and designed for a very specific set of purposes.

In addition to such concepts, there are a large number that we can call general concepts, widely used within and without specialist domains. They are used to flex a large number of concerns and seem to have meaning in some independence of what they are linked to. These include *not, and, but, if, because, never, implies, numbers, who,* and many more. These concepts are everywhere, and some of them have been described in detail by logicians who have been concerned to give an account of their powers in effecting inferences. It is important to remember that not everything making up our speech and thought is historical and hence of only limited and passing worth. Aristotle and other logicians of the ancient past were intent upon describing many of the concepts that were not affected by material considerations and the issues at hand. The notion that logic is a formal discipline rests in large part upon the recognition that many concepts invoked and described in logic have properties that outlast whatever we talk about in this day or that. Concepts like "object," "event," "thing," and others are like that. For our purposes it is not necessary to decide if formal and logical concepts are eternal or if they have some kind of *ens rationis* that accounts for their endurance. It is enough here only to note that these expressions and their roles arise again and again, and that both vernacular and specialist ways of talking and reasoning seem to bring them forth.

We also have concepts that are loosely descriptive, that categorize and describe very general features of our common life. Grammatical concepts, for example, refer to very general features of language, which features persist and make grammar one of the oldest and most abiding of disciplines. Logic is something like that, too, as is what Aristotle called "rhetoric." Large category words, by which we distinguish hot from cold, easy from hard, rough from smooth, humans from animals, rulers from ruled—these also have an endurance that is striking. I cite these only to discredit the prevailing idea that all concepts are in flux and/or timebound. This is loosely said when we argue that all concepts are historical, meaning apparently that every concept has its origin, prevails awhile, then passes out of use. Of course, some concepts are of only temporary significance. "Phlogiston" is no longer of any use to chemists; neither are "humors" to physiologists; and "instincts" are clearly no longer the major concern of psychologists. The life seems to be gone from most of these, and now it takes an historical interest to see what vitality they once did have. However, there was a time when their vitality was assured by scientific activity itself. Now it takes an historical imagination, at the very least. Notions like "transubstantiation" and "real presence" and a few others are a bit like that in theology, too.

We are led to believe from some very obvious instances that all concepts must have the same kind of careers. That is, we are led very quickly to a theory that proposes to tell us something about all concepts, if not all words, at once. If a man from Mars heard us calling to our children, "Come and look at the beautiful sunset!", he might be surprised; for he had probably read a great deal about earth people and learned that they had become Copernican in their astronomy. This meant, he knew, that they now believed that the earth was a planet moving around the sun. Therefore, the sun did not move but only appeared to do so. So how was he to account for a parent's persistence in talking about sunrises? Being very wise, he says nothing, but he listens carefully. Sure enough, a day later, he hears that the sun set at 7:53 P.M., and a meteorologist is reported to have said this. Because of what he had read, he assumed that the concepts "sunset" and "sunrise" were outmoded and that a new and comprehensive way of speaking had replaced the old way. That is the way the replacement of the Ptolemaic astronomy by the Copernican had been described in the textbook used on Mars.

The man from Mars was mistaken and the book misleading. Though it is true that one astronomy has replaced another, it is not true that all the concepts he had heard were theory-saturated. Nor were all older concepts replaced. Despite the view he had imbibed, it is not true that concepts like "sunset" and "sunrise" were replaced by other and better ones. For those expressions were not really theory-words nor theory-concepts every time they were used. Insofar as they called attention to very striking happenings, they still do so, Copernicus notwithstanding. When one made them do service for the theoretical job of explaining the universe as astronomers have wanted to do, then those concepts simply failed. Furthermore, one kind of picture we are tempted to draw for ourselves with these concepts is plainly wrong. For the sun does not move around at all. But the concept "sunrise" need not deceive; and for those who understand the newer astronomy, there is still no mistake being made when parents call their children to see the sunrise. The expression still has power as it always did, but it does not have the power now of suggesting a comprehensive theory about heavenly motion. One must stop somewhere with every concept.

Some concepts, then, have an enduring life even when they have been rejected for certain theoretical purposes. Their vitality goes on, and not only in metaphorical and figurative senses, either. For those very concepts are not metaphorical in all cases, though we can well imagine them being used metaphorically, too. However, my interest is not here at all. Instead, I want to stress the fact that not all concepts wax and wane, live and die, so that we cannot say blandly about them, as a class, that they are all historical. That theory is wrong. That generalization is too sweeping and stifles our sensing many differences. Most of the concepts that inform our esthetic, moral, and religious concerns have a striking nonhistorical character about them. Again, we do not have to insist that they are eternal in order to establish that they are neither like a "rash" nor a "vogue," nor simply sophisticated ideas now sadly outmoded.

For it is also true that some concepts have a nonhistorical character about them. By the term *nonhistorical*, I do not suggest anything ethereal or otherworldly. Rather, I am only drawing attention to the fact that the concept does not need any particular historical surrounding in order for it to acquire vitality. All or any historical settings are sufficient. The familiar concept "I," which all of us use, is a typical one. It never was a technical concept, and thus never was born in a specialist context. It is not to be confused with what philosophers and others were looking for when they wrote about the transcendental ego and "personal identity." These are specialist inquiries and do not infringe markedly upon (nor even trade upon) the use of the expression *I*. We did not learn the use of the word *I* by any such overt teaching. No one has defined the word for us or given us special warrant for it. Its established function is not in need of any justification whatsoever. Not only is the concept widespread, but it is neither old-fashioned nor new. It has a kind of use that does not beg sanctions from learning, old or new. One cannot imagine what kind of learning would ever render it out of date. No one seems to make mistakes with it, except children who are just learning to talk. Sometimes they get confused into thinking that *you* and *me* and *I* are like names and must not be used by just anybody to refer but only by the person they first heard use them. Then they treat them like labels, not concepts. But this kind of mistake is easily corrected, usually by the child himself.

Some concepts, like "I," are very general in use. Everybody who talks has the concept. Surely this kind of concept has such a nonhistorical and persistent employment because it conforms with a general fact. There are such things as persons; and there are such things as persons who talk about themselves. The word *I* expresses a general fact, and hence it helps us to comprehend and gives a us a way of dealing with situations in which we are involved.

V

Some of the concepts of the Christian faith have a correspondence, too, with general facts. Therefore, such concepts as "faith" and "God" are not arbitrary inventions, cast up in order to make people perform in a certain way. For "faith" has to do with a range of uncertainties, on the one side, and the human need for resolving one's fate amid these uncertainties on the other. Again, that concept was not brought about by epistemologists nor by theologians. It springs forth whenever people become preoccupied with what is right before their noses. So, too, that strange concept, "God." It has been with the race as long as we can mark human history, but just what facts, psychological or physical, it corresponds to, even in the most general way, has been long disputed. My point is not to resolve that dispute but only to argue that such a concept is not a wild fabrication, whatever else it may be. It was not invented and then imposed by fiat or custom upon the unwilling. It is more stubborn and deeper than that. "God" has an odd fittingness over the centuries. Our point is not, however, to stress whatever are the facts to which "God" might correspond, but to remark upon the concept. For having the concept "God" is also to have a certain set of functions in one's life. If one knows how to use the word *God* in prayer and worship, then one has the concept. One can do all sorts of things with that concept "God"— for example, one can explain, praise, and curse. One can even attain peace of mind and forgiveness of sin. The concept is crucial to a way of life and a view of life. My point is that the concept is not indigenous to only one time, place, period, or people. Where praising and praying are done, the concept "God" is operative, and people can be said to already have it, even if they are not defining it or overtly discussing it. "God," as a concept, has a kind of location and place in our lives. It has some connections and not others. It does something and not everything. Furthermore, it is almost primitive, and much of a religious life is based upon it. It is often the genesis rather than the result of our religious thinking, but even that proposal has to be said very guardedly.

Christian concepts, along with many of those associated with the religion of the Jews, are variously exercised. One might put the matter in a most extreme form by saying that if one is being made humble, contrite, poor in spirit, and pure in heart, then Christian concepts are already in command. And if one learns to walk according to the new teachings of Christ, the Apostle Paul tells us, we will not be walking according to the course of this world but in dramatically new ways. These he outlines in remarks addressed to the Christians in Ephesus. The Christian life is not something that can be charted and described once and for all for everyone. The reason for this brings us again to our topic. Just as we learn words and sometimes phrases of a new language in order to write paragraphs and books, and just as we learn old words to say new things, so Christians have to acquire some things, among them emotions, virtues, and also those capacities we have called concepts, in order to live Christian lives. One needs to know how to love, to hope, and what to believe—all of these taken together begin to provide the conditions by which a person can forge his or her own life in a manner that is distinctively Christian.

Not all concepts are equal because we lump them so unceremoniously in one big group called "concepts." Some are more important than others. For example, the concept "God" is a very diffuse and deep one. It arises in strange ways. It crops up in strange expressions that pervade everyday speech. "God help us," people say in dire circumstances. And Jesus and his teachings lead one to identify God and worship him, almost as if the former is a means to the latter. All sorts of factors give the concept "God" a kind of foreboding and somewhat obsidian character. "God" is linked with the "unknown," what is unutterable, the limits of our speech, the beginning of everything, the goal of everything, etc. Admittedly, these expressions invite vagueness and a mad splurge of speculation, but they also are fitting, under guarded circumstances, for genuine human feelings of helplessness, limitation, guilt, and frustration. "God," as a concept, is a dark one indeed, born sometimes out of incongruities and black despair. To believe in God is like finding a little hope when all is depressing around you; to trust in God is like taking heart when you seem to have no right to it. These are minimal surroundings for the concept "God" that make it vital. And Christianity does not always introduce the concept "God," though it may in some instances. Most of the time, Christian teachings trade upon it, modifying it by reference to the person of Jesus and extending it to all kinds of additional circumstances.

There is a sense in which a person already has the concept of "self" or "I" if he or she can use the first-person pronoun correctly. One need not also be able to talk about the concept or to define it in an ostensible manner. A successful use is a sufficient sign of mastery. So, too, the Christian concepts enable persons to speak faithfully and strongly about the world in which they live. How they get the concepts in the first place may be another matter altogether. There is a language of faith that is not only a sign of faith but also a part of faith. To speak *about* that language of faith is an achievement of scholarship and one form of theologizing; but to speak so that those concepts authorize one's speech as they did for St. Paul in his grandiloquent hymn of love, or as they did for Mary in what we know as the "Magnificat"— these are to use the concepts and not to talk about them. But other achievements are to be expected, too. The kind of joyous life, triumphant over hunger, sword, and even death, replete with a powerful enthusiasm that conquers the circumstances rather than being conquered by them—this is surely as much a work of these Christian components as is more speaking. But it is difficult to say just which powers are conceptual and which are something else. Christians are expected to respond to the novelties of life, literally to play the game of life, in a distinctive way. For everything in Christian teaching, the most abstruse theological matters and the most specific forms of charity and faith, are entangled with all kinds of moral considerations and with emotions, too. So one learns affections and passions, and these likewise empower one in subsequent circumstances. The admonitions about putting on the new man (Ephesians 4) certainly suggest that some specific righteous achievements—telling the truth, talking clean, along with knowing God through Christ—can link up so that one is armed for a truly Christlike life. The capacities are not exclusively conceptual, to be sure, but they include conceptual capacities.

Other passages in Scripture describe what it means to have the mind of Christ Jesus. Many things are said about this that could be summarized somewhat as follows. It is as if a human being can

have a new kind of consciousness. Anyone of us can learn to
intend and to address the world in altogether a new way. Rather
than assuming that this word *consciousness* entails a kind of
spooky essence somehow living in the brain, let me hasten to note
that I am using the word *conscious* here in a very plain way.
When one smiles *at* something, not vacantly, then one is using a
smile with propriety. It becomes part of a significant motley of
behavior. It goes with language, with deeds, with a person.
Laughs, cries, gestures, words, looks, glances, emotions, feelings—
all of these can be wrong, inept, empty, or inappropriate. When
there is some kind of rightness or appropriateness about these acts,
so that one is not just doing them but doing something *with* them,
then we say that a person is conscious. One must feel something,
not just have his or her eyes open. One must cry about something,
for otherwise endless crying is a sign that something else is wrong.
Considering these examples, we can say that being conscious is a
matter of making our acts responsible. It is to hook up mental and
other acts with persons, places, and things.

However, it is not enough to say that being a Christian is only
a matter of being conscious. For the manner of being conscious is
what matters here. Being a Christian is also describable as a
"how," not only a "what." There is a way to love, hope, care,
respond, be joyful, and be sorrowful that is tied up very intimately
with the "what." The "what" is ordinarily proposed in judgments
about God and the world—what we have been calling theology.
The "how" is, in part, a nonverbal way to employ the same
components that make the judgments possible. This is not a matter
of thoughts being expressed in action; rather, what authorizes
thoughts also authorizes, even requires, nonverbal behavior. Emotions, feelings, acts of mercy, confidence, hope for daily life—
these and more are equally ingredient. The "how" can also be said
to sometimes come before the "what"; and our reason for saying
this is simply the Scripture itself, which shows how the theological
teachings (and some parts thereof) on some occasions followed the
acquisition of the "how." It is unfortunate that theology has been

likened to "theory" and daily living to "practice," thus crediting
the absurd notion that theology always precedes the nonverbal
faithful living. No, these matters are very complex; sometimes one
is first, sometimes another. For one person, the teachings come
prior, but others learn the faith via the law and a kind of
obedience.

It is a mistake to formalize the pedagogy too closely. The
typical way of getting people in on the business of Christianity is
through the story of Jesus and his career, including his birth, life,
death, and resurrection. But this is not the only possible way. The
New Testament describes all sorts of ways in which people
become oriented to what is later called Christianity. Some people
respond to a request, some obey a specific command, some
appreciate in a profound way what Jesus has done, some express
contrition and ask for forgiveness. The New Testament itself
weaves these together into a complex account that the churches
have been using ever since. That story, plus an additional number
of letters of early Apostles, includes a motley of themes, admonitions, pieces of narrative, and judgments about this and that. The
point I wish to make here is that pieces of that story can be
learned and appreciated by a later hearer so that he reduplicates
some of the behavior of the persons in the original drama. Those
components can still produce the ability to think as sweepingly
and sharply of the world as the original protagonists did (this
might then look like making a later reader "theological"); they
can reproduce the passionate enthusiasm all over again that
gripped the Apostle Paul; they can stir the bare bones of a
twentieth-century reader into unexpected virtues and moral sensi-
tivity; they can create emotions like hope, guilt, and joy.

It is hard to say, for all instances, what comes first and what
comes second. But Kierkegaard, arguing for the distinctiveness of
Christian emotions, makes a relevant point:

Emotion which is Christian is checked by the definition of concepts, and
when emotion is transposed or expressed in words in order to be
communicated, this transposition must occur constantly within the defini-

tion of the concepts. . . . In order to express oneself Christianly there is required, besides the more universal language of the heart, also skill and schooling in the definition of Christian concepts, while at the same time it is of course assumed that the emotion is of a specific, qualitative sort, the Christian emotion.[3]

Sometimes the emotions are aroused first, as Kierkegaard showed in his study of how human beings despair. To someone already in despair, the Christian teachings then begin to speak; and the interlocking of teachings and emotion, concepts and pathos, takes a different order. At other times, the teachings precipitate despair and guilt, and another sequence then prevails. In either case, the relation between a "how" and a "what" is intimate.

My point, however, is to draw further attention to what is the normal range of expectations attaching to religious teachings— and most especially to religious concepts. To teach these to people, no matter where, ghettos or suburbs, requires a comprehension of the range of ramifications. But the range is not all-inclusive. Neither is it random or fortuitous. The range includes the acquisition of new and very tough and resilient emotions—like hope (instead of despair), a kind of affection for other people (instead of mistrust and dislike of them), and even peace (instead of the nervous anxiety gnawing away at one's little confidences). These things are called "fruits of the spirit" in a typical bit of New Testament parlance.

But there is more. Just as religious concepts help one to see the world differently, as if it were God's and as if one were not alone, so they produce a new emotional tone appropriate to that appraisal of things. Also, new ways of disposing oneself towards the world and its problems are equally required. The new concepts also engender new determinations of virtues and vices, not only drawing the line between them differently, but also generating

Søren Kierkegaard, *On Authority and Revelation*, trans. Walter Lowrie (Princeton, 1955), pp. 163–164.

virtues appropriate to the situations in which men find themselves. This does not commit one to "situation-ethics," but it does
limn the way in which religious teachings work. Of course, just as
the religious emotions are part of the appraisal of the human
scene—the world can be a dreadful or a hopeful place—so, too,
can those emotions become part of the action appropriate to that
world. Thus the teachings get bound up with attitudes, feelings,
passions, and a host of behavior patterns, not indiscriminately, but
in patterned ways.

However, the point in saying all of this was to note that
religious concepts do all kinds of things. They allow us to speak
about the world and God in a variety of ways, and that is part of
what theology becomes. This is a typical linguistic use of the
concepts, not to be denied its role but not to be praised as the
supreme exercise thereof, either. For there are all kinds of other
requisites in the religious life. When those religious concepts are
proposed in an appropriate context and with due weight given
them, then humility, contrition, repentance, hope, love, and joy
are also demanded. These are part of, not just applications of, the
force of these concepts. They are difficult to teach, and the
teaching here involves something much more like training than it
does imparting information. A kind of nurture is needed, not just
a kind of publicity. One gets to see as well as understand the
world differently. Different feelings about one's tasks develop,
and a radically new composure towards the world—a contrasting
metaphysics—is also elicited.

8

Theology, Atheism, and Theism

The cluster of views which we call "theism" is almost invariably associated with Christianity and Judaism (less often with most other religions). Many educated people are convinced that "theism" is the diagnosis and statement of the concepts already basic and elemental in one's thinking and behavior if one is conventionally religious. To get at such concepts is the task of technically trained students, but the task is of importance not just to them but to everyone.

Being religious is what one might call a first-level kind of activity. Perhaps it is something like being a scientist, or maybe an educator, or even a historian. In all of these latter endeavors, one indulges a range of intellectual activities. One learns to speak in the scientific manner about what one hopes are the facts of the matter. So, too, with the historical account, there is a game to be learned and a way and manner to promulgate it and size up the states of affairs from within it. In respect to all of these games, there is another kind of activity possible. One can think out a philosophy of science and a kind of philosophy of history, too. These are attempts to lay bare the methodologies, the presuppositions, the concepts, the axioms, the tacit beliefs, and perhaps other antecedent factors that are deemed to be present.

The philosophy of science ostensibly gets at something that is "in" science but that is not the same as the subject matter of scientific inquiry. And the philosophies of art, education, history, and even mathematics, along with other equally specialized studies, purport to work out components that are said to be present, yet not quite explicit and clear. It is as if there were a conceptual background, accessible only to philosophical tools, against which these activities take place. In religious circles, theism is credited with being that conceptual ground. Part of the lament widely heard today is justified; for when it is said that theism is no longer relevant to science, art, history, etc., this is to remark upon the fact that most of these endeavors certainly do not depend upon a common metaphysical scheme and certainly not upon theism. The notion that there was a common and universal conceptual scheme, equally relevant to all intellectual and humane endeavors, is a large part of the enthusiasm for a metaphysics. Today we are not quite so sure of that singular scheme. Instead, there seem to be philosophical schemes in the plural, one for each kind of domain, and they have, in turn, rather little in common. Early statements of theism, like St. Thomas's, made all of learning appear to depend in subtle ways upon something metaphysical, which if not theistic was yet compatible with Christianity and other positive religious teachings and became equally ingredient in all kinds of learned domains.

For better or for worse, theism is still talked about as a kind of conceptual scheme. The claims made for it are widespread, long-established, and plausible—but plausible only if one does not examine them in great detail. Besides, theism is said to be fundamental to Christianity, Judaism, and Islam, as well as to many other convictional outlooks of the world. Though religions otherwise differ, it has been widely declared that they share this theistic scheme of concepts. Theism looks like a religion-neutral philosophical context within which one can discern common fundamentals.

Nonetheless, this theistic system, too, has come in for very serious criticism. All of us know about alternative schemes some of which are clearly atheistic. Lucretius, Hobbes, Hume, Voltaire, materialists, determinists of certain kinds, positivists, and others have proposed substitute schemes. Atheisms are of diverse sorts, but one is an atheist (relative to theism) however one denies that theistic scheme. For a long while now, the problem of science versus religion has been leading some people to say that the conceptual scheme of science is atheistic, or if not that, at least nontheistic; and the incompatibility between science and religion has had more to do with the reputed philosophical bearings of each than with the respective claims of the religious and scientific teachings. Also, the very fact that this conflict between science and religion takes so many forms (psychological versus theological accounts of man, biological versus Biblical descriptions of living things and their origins) brings out the point already made— namely, that there is no prevailing common metaphysical scheme holding between them. Nontheistic concepts are, because of science, more popular and more widely espoused today than heretofore. But this brings us to the heart of the matter.

In the pages that follow, I wish to argue that the theism/atheism issue is a pseudo-issue and that the issues covered by that rubric must be otherwise handled even to make sense, let alone to be resolved. Furthermore, I will try to show that theism, in its pretentious philosophical sense, is not fundamental to Judaism and Christianity; and that the denials of theism—even conceptual atheisms—are not necessarily denials of Christianity and Judaism. It will be suggested, in addition, that this negative case is not a warrant for saying that modern religion must be without God. In short, if the argument proposed is valid, then it should be clear that even some of the new sophisticated existential and ontological theologies, which propose atheistical or nontheistical conceptual schemes, are largely irrelevant. Their mistakes are logical, not factual. The point, crucial to all of the rest, is simply that no such ⟵ conceptual scheme is needed at all. There are concepts enough, rich ones too, already operative in religious life and practice, and to make these clear would be more than a life's work for a theologian. Furthermore, it should be obvious in what follows that there is a way to talk about God's existence and his love and care

of the world without thereby insisting upon the system ordinarily
called theism.

Theism, which is claimed to be the conceptual ground of some
religions, actually does justice to none. Besides being too general
and having a smothering effect upon the peculiarities of Christian, Jewish, and other positive beliefs, the very logical moves
constituting it are dubious.

I I

Philosophical theism, despite its long and hallowed history, is
not the essence of Christian and Jewish religion; neither is the
denial of that theism invariably and necessarily the denial of God
Almighty. The point is, rather, that theism is not the standard and
ineluctable conceptual part, there to be discovered every time one
undoes faith by intellectual analysis. To deny that it is standard is
not to say much of anything.

Through the centuries, it has become a very complicated
matter either to defend or to attack, for example, Christianity. For
the theistic contention is that the concepts making up theism are
the essence of Christianity. Until one isolates theism and positively
countermands it, one cannot even be a respectable critic of the
Christian religion. On both sides, the attack and the defense, the
task becomes terribly abstract. There is something absurd about
this. Crucifying Jesus, living faithlessly, and loving the world with
all one's heart, soul, mind, and strength tend then to become
trivialities compared to denying theism. It is almost as if the
academics have made crucial what was not so initially. Nonetheless, the theist will have us believe that to deny God's existence
and the things said about him somehow are profoundly involved
in doing all of the above things, just as he will have us believe that
in following Jesus, behaving faithfully, and obeying the first
commandment are contained the theistic concepts.

Put in another way, a defense of the faith is complicated. For
obedience and following, loyalty and suffering, even for Jesus'

sake, are all thought to be by-products of, or in some way consequents to, the more fundamental matter of believing in theism. Therefore, theism is what counts and what must be defended at all costs, whereas the specific sins and works of unrighteousness, of which Jesus and Paul speak so often as if they are to be avoided above all else, become too small even to mention. Christians (and one might include certain Jews and certain followers of Mohammed, among others) have accordingly been pledged to defend the existence of a kind of nonnatural realm, including God, vast purposes, indestructible values, and a lot else besides, which realm is only penetrable by the help of special philosophical and theological concepts. This tissue of sophisticated talk is said, besides, to describe reality and to be the very ground of everything in the life of faith. All of this has to do with "being," and lately with the "ground" of being.

Some years ago, a distinguished British philosopher, Gilbert Ryle, began to analyze the concept of "mind."[1] The word *mind* obviously is woven into the tapestry of our language, popular and technical. But the aim of Ryle's book was not to dislodge the word from our usage, but to examine the attempts of philosophers to take that word and show its spiritual referent, mind itself. For this is what concepts most often do, when properly used—namely, refer to something or other. However, Professor Ryle shows his readers that the nonmaterial, mental stuff called mind is a "gratuitous personification of an habitual way in which a human being acts." This "mind" is what he refers to sarcastically as "the ghost in the machine."

One need not grant Ryle every point in his book in order to recognize the merits of what is a major thrust. He is hard after a kind of metaphysics that keeps sneaking in and making us overlook the subtleties and multitudinous ways of thinking, feeling, and talking that our daily life entails. A metaphysical concern for "mind" and for big "category" words (like *consciousness,*

---

[1] Gilbert Ryle, *The Concept of Mind* (London, 1962). See especially pp. 15 ff.

emotions, and *thoughts)* causes the neglect of the little details of
our natural everyday discourse and awareness. Certainly his book
does not deprive us of the right to say: "Her mind was destroyed"
or "He has a good mind." For this referential, everyday, and
common usage can be a highly significant one, if the language is
careful and the surroundings right. It need not obligate one to a
spiritual conception of mental life or to a dualistic metaphysics.

Today we are quite accustomed to an empirical kind of
psychology that describes behavior, including our thinking, without involving special metaphysical concepts like "mind," "soul,"
"faculties," and the rest.[2] So, too, other sciences are no longer
dependent upon "entelechies," "substance," "being," and "potencies," once the peculiar province of transcendental insight and
description. But theology—certainly that which pretends to be
constructive, perhaps systematic, and exciting—is aimed at the
task of giving one additional knowledge of an immaterial and
divine realm. So much is this the case that most of philosophical
and second-hand theology today is twisting about, this way and
that, to refurbish those persistent philosophical concepts with a
meaning that is viable and tough for our twentieth century.

In America, many earnest theologians are trying to give the
concept of "God" meaning by suggesting that A. N. Whitehead's
philosophical categories and concepts—metaphysical with a vengeance—will refurbish the theistic apparatus. Others, in Europe
and America, are using the speculative biology of Teilhard de
Chardin; and still others, the new sophisticated logics which look
like a respectable way to reinstate Plato's ideal entities. Europe-
ans, too, have discovered in Heidegger and Jaspers, "being,"
"existence," and other ontological concepts. It is no longer a secret

---

[2] One has to be very careful here, however. Many of the sciences today,
including psychology, all too quickly get rid of one kind of metaphysics and then
quickly espouse another like "behaviorism" or kinds of materialism. Some matters
are more subtle. Notions of "general law," "explanation," "causality," and others
often introduce the metaphysical issues in disguised form. But these matters must
be addressed separately.

that theologians were once greatly indebted to idealistic metaphysics; for whatever else one might say about the kinds of
idealists, they did propose a scheme of concepts that marked what
looked like the necessary, universal, and persistent features of our
world. It was an easy step from such a scheme to the theological
conviction that here were the bases and stuff for one's knowledge
of God. Without this idealistic conceptual scheme, most theologians today have no way to be "theistic" or even to claim the
intellectualistic position which they think theology must avow if it
is to be knowledge at all.

There is something to the charge that most of this theistic
metaphysics—whether time-honored idealism, scholasticism, other kinds of supernaturalism, or modern "process," logistical, or
ontological schemes—is really a lot of nonsense. Certainly, we do
not know how to argue the rightness or wrongness of such views;
for they are arbitrary and loosely related to the everyday world.
Worse than that, though, is the fact that most of theistic metaphysics is as meaningless to contemporaries as the talk about
invisible spirits and "anima" indwelling in trees and waters is to
the students of botany and geology. Thus far, surely, there is a
glorious intellectual irrelevance about theism, for it simply does
not illuminate the world we live in or give substance to religious
thinking. Instead, it looks—whether in old or new forms, whether
Heideggerian, Whiteheadian, Platonic, or Rahnerian—like a gratuitous invention.

Besides that, theism is not a definitive analysis and depiction
of what is involved in most Jewish and Christian thinking.
Students of Biblical literature in our time have produced a serious
rift in the ranks by insisting that the conceptual scheme investing
the Scripture with worth is that of *Heilsgeschichte*, or "holy
history." So-called Biblical theology, therefore, has produced in
our century quite a different set of concepts from that of
traditional theism, and these new notions are still said to get at the
essence of Biblical religion. My point is not to praise this effort; for
it, too, is another schematism satisfying a metaphysical urge

rather than actually illuminating much of anything. But whenever the theistic theologian insists that theistic concepts are the
disclosure of what is involved in the Bible, it is well to remind him
or her of the presence of the theologian of *Heilsgeschichte*. Both
schemes have, in fact, a touch of the arbitrary about them; and
this realization ought to impel us, instead of looking for a scheme
of concepts, to look at ourselves and examine rather closely this
intense desire for another more intellectual set of concepts. We all
seem to be discontent with the concepts that the language of faith
already provides. Yet, in the latter only is our hope for being
emboldened to a life of faith and some thoughts with real
integrity.

I I I

There is no denying that theism is extremely subtle. The irony
is that an attack upon theism seems also to be an attack upon the
work of some of the most skillful and intellectually talented
proponents of religious faith. Theistic theology even looks like a
kind of religion-neutral spiritual knowledge, fundamental to all of
the rest of religion, and ecumenical with a vengeance.

Being a theist as opposed to being an atheist purports to be an
intellectual matter, something independent of being a Christian, a
Jew, or what have you. On the other hand, being a Christian or a
Jew or what have you binds one inextricably, it is said, to being a
kind of theist. Theism is a "genus" word, and the positive religions
and their theologies are like species within that genus. Recently,
new ways of connecting these things have been invented. Being a
Christian, for example, is said to be a matter that is often unclear
and unanalyzed. One frequently does not know what it "means"
to be a Christian, it is purported, until one gets at the concepts
that are involved. This matter of connecting up concepts with
"meaning" is another strange and subtle relation, quite tempting
to intellectually oriented people. However, it is by no means
obvious, even though it is widely held, that all meanings are made

clear by intellectual analyses; nor is it clear, either, that all concepts are, for that matter, intellectualistic and only the names for abstract bits of *ens rationis*.[2]

There is, however, this new use for theism—namely, to serve as the ultimate court of meaning, and also as the skein of reality to which *God, Spirit,* and other big religious words must refer. The charge is widely made that theism in our day has become meaningless because those big words and other long Latinate abstract nouns—*regeneration, temptation, resignation, consecration, sanctification*—tangled up in the theistic net, no longer mean anything. Therefore, some theologians have urged that we be atheistic, while others (like Tillich and Heidegger) have urged that we get rid of the dichotomous way of thinking—God "in" being or God *not* "in" being—and identify God altogether differently. Perhaps as being itself or as the ground of being. In all these cases, "meaning" is still the goal; and the thesis is that a better set of concepts is needed to state the meanings or even to get the meanings launched.

It is a little difficult to oppose this. Any kind of opposition looks anti-intellectual and like a vote for plebeian piety. But the point of our analysis is not to make a case for grossness nor to veto logic and analytic skill. Neither is any kind of disparagement of abstract reflection intended. On the contrary, it can be asserted that the most detailed and seemingly disinterested analysis is very frequently also the most useful. Great detail and great skill are essential to becoming clear. Furthermore, religions, not least Christianity, do live in part by concepts, and these, in turn, become muddied by dubious associations and are frequently misconstrued by virtue of their resemblances to concepts found in the sciences, in esthetics, and surely in morals. So the opposition here is not to the application of intellectual skills to religious affairs but rather to the odd intellectualist and quasi-metaphysical position that is difficult to ferret out and difficult, too, to state.

---

[3] Another kind of account of concepts was given in the previous chapter.

This intellectualist view is no longer argued and is seldom, therefore, made explicit. Of course, it probably is not (and never was) an arguable matter and thereby shows, besides, that it is somewhat arbitrary. Nonetheless, the conviction is powerful and causes us to look for all kinds of wrong things, to expect more than intelligence can ever proffer, and, generally, to misplace a wide range of problems and issues. Theism plays a large role in an intellectualist economy. Even people who have no regard for religious faith take it to be a matter of course that anyone who does take it seriously must therefore be a theist. On the other hand, the person who is not religious and who is an intellectual will most frequently say that he or she is an atheist, neglecting to mention, perhaps, that one is actually and instead a blasphemer, or indifferent, or lazy, or insensitive, or plainly disinclined, or any number of other things that a person can be by way of being nonreligious.

The point here is that theism is not an imposition. Rather, it fits a kind of academic prejudice and conviction quite handily. For one can be a theist without being otherwise religious, and one can be an atheist without being an irrationalist; but one seemingly cannot be neither a theist nor an atheist without a breach with the minimal conditions of rationality. For the academic prejudice here baldly stated is that if one is neither a theist nor an atheist, he does not care at all about how religious talk is grounded. It is as if theism/atheism is a serious affair and involves making up your mind on the ultimates. The dichotomy tends to exhaust the possibilities.

Perhaps this can be qualified a bit. It has been decreed for a long while that the dichotomy exhausted the rational options. But then came those who said theism and atheism are not quite exhaustive—for in both "God exists" and "God does not exist," the working assumption was that the first meant "God is in being" and the second "God is not in being." A note of the great idealist spiritual tradition has been sounded recently in Jaspers, Heidegger, Tillich, and numerous of their followers—namely, that God is not "in" being, but rather that he *is* being. Therefore neither *exists* nor *does not exist* applies to him at all. It is no wonder, then, that this kind of philosophizing seems to some people to be the hope for theology's being saved as a kind of knowledge, and to be a new and stout answer to the world's doubters. But the academic prejudice is still at work; for this kind of theology still has to ground everyday religious language and practice in something that only philosophical concepts can possibly reach. This "new" move is not radical at all—it merely restates the academic prejudice in another form.

This prejudice is very easy to succumb to. Most of the time, we think "with" ideas and "about" the world and a host of things. Only under special circumstances do we think about ideas. Ordinarily, all concepts, ideas, percepts, sensations, and the rest are "of" things, people, and places, and include what is called "reference" as part of their use and meaning. But a long-standing prejudice in Western intellectual circles has made us think that ideas or concepts are purely mental and only in the mind, and that their reference to anything outside of the mind requires another kind of intellectual job. Philosophical "isms" or schemes, conceptual to be sure, are necessary to show that ideas refer to something. And philosophical concepts always look like a promising way to get at the spiritual stuff where the ordinary language fails.

In religious contexts, this academic prejudice works in the following way. It can be admitted that first-level and ordinary religious beliefs and behavior produce and evince a wide array of concepts—"grace," "God," "love," "forgiveness," "faith," and numerous others. But it is believed that these concepts are, within the kind of context, uncertain, and in an exceedingly subtle way. For there is supposedly a real point to the question: Is there or is there not a God? Ordinary language supposedly treats matters "as if" there were a God, but doubts will creep in. Theism becomes both the way of treating the meaning of the term *God,* and thus of grounding it in its proper referent, and also the way of treating the question whether anything exists to which such a concept can refer.

The prejudice of which I have spoken is a prejudice of the learned and is therefore fiendishly difficult to eradicate. In part, this prejudicial proclivity was the target of Wittgenstein's *Philosophical Investigations,* as well as the subject of many of Kierkegaard's diatribes against the supposed dependence of Christianity upon philosophical and psychological concepts. This prejudice works to effect a separation between ideas, as if they were psychical, intellectual, and spiritual, and their referents, as if they must be of a different genre and quality. Clearly, most of the problems that philosophers try to resolve for religious men (as well as when they try to "ground" politics, science, morals, etc.) are created by conceiving of matters in this bifurcating way. Of course, the duality has to be overcome. In religious circles, theism, with its assertions that there is a God with such and such characteristics, seems to tell us that, after all, there just might be something to which Biblical authors were referring and that there may be something on which to ground popular religion. The ordinary language of faith is thought to need a foundation and another learned formulation.

My point all along has been that this kind of learning is really a pseudo-learning. The concepts within such discourse as theism (or its modern substitutes) are invariably artificial anyway and have no real work to do except that provided by those who think them up. This is why there are so many alternative systems built around these ostensibly important matters and also why there is no limit to the number that can be proposed. It is only conceivability" and nothing else that finally puts restraints upon the enterprises. Furthermore, the concepts in the theistic schemes are not genuine concepts. For example, the concept of God as "first cause" is not an analysis of God as described in the first few chapters of Genesis; so there is little obvious connection, if any, between the two concepts. But more, the concept of "first cause" has little working significance; for insofar as it trades on the general concept of "cause," it turns out that there is no general working concept. All concepts of "cause" occur only within specific domains, and they seem to be quite different therein. The generalized concept was a philosophical creation and is another instance of an almost useless and overgeneralized concept. To add "first" to it, whether "primary" or "first in time," is to compound the verbiage but not much else. But those words also have to be concepts; they survive because their working context is the very philosophical prose in which they are created.

This is the intellectual stuff with which the theism/atheism issues are ensnared. It is about time that Christian theologians, let alone the philosophers, stop inventing concepts that work only in contrived contexts, and begin to study those we already have. We already have a working language of faith. We do not need "theism." Neither do we need substitutes for theism. For our point is that neither affirming nor denying theism is an important matter. Philosophically it is a kind of gratuitous business; religiously it is simply trivial. And I suspect the same can be said about other schemes, early and late, that try to replace the theistic apparatus. Theism once purported to be the understanding of, for example, Christianity. Clearly, today, theism is itself something to understand. It has become not an aid to understanding but that which must be explained, proved, justified, and clarified before it can itself be understood. Therefore, the critics are right when they say that theism is not viable any longer. But I am here pushing matters even further by insisting that we are wrong in assuming that an intellectual scheme like theism (or its substitutes) is needed at all.

Logically, the notion that we must have a conceptual philosophical scheme in order to understand is a howler. For if we do not understand, we sometimes need explanations, training, information, skills, and patient teachers. The assertion that philosophical theism is the "understanding" of Christianity can only be a downright mistake. For finally there is no ultimate court of understanding. Furthermore, even Biblical language *was* the understanding of some people, and one must recover the conditions for understanding that language not by creating another one, but by understanding with it.

I V

Instead of the theism/atheism issue, we must once more return to the common ways of speaking about God, grace, Jesus, and Spirit, and to the common ways of behaving that Scripture enjoins. There are, clearly enough, a host of difficulties in doing either. But one thing we must avoid above all else, and that is the perpetual and restless philosophical seeking for knowledge about God. This drives us to neglect doing even what we can and ought to do and to attempt what in principle cannot satisfy us. Most people of any academic pretensions, also exposed to Christianity, soon forsake altogether trying to obey Jesus or Paul, let alone other admonitions of their church and literature, and begin instead to try to "understand" the teachings. Then they are off. Stirred by an insatiable curiosity, and kept envious by vague notions of perfect knowledge and infallible facts, each reflective person progressively reduces his claims to know and then his ability to act. All of this becomes an intellectual virtue. Agnosticism about some things becomes agnosticism about all things—God, reality, and everything the church teaches. The long pursuit for a limited but invulnerable knowledge of God has then begun. Philosophic doubt has begun, and only a theism—a scheme of rather precise but generalized concepts, logically a little more pure—promises surcease.

Fortunately, there are primitive credenda that keep us sensible. Both David Hume and J. G. Hamann noted how these reasserted themselves the moment one takes up again the affairs of daily life or speaks the everyday language. Surely, being a Christian has much more to do with "how" one takes up the affairs of everyday life than it does with glimpsing into transnatural realms, more to do with loving neighbors than with a reality to which they are unwitting testimonies, and more to do with common sense than with a finespun system making it dubious. However, the doubter wants more than "how," more than the admonition to love, more than commands and parables, stories and recommendations. It is as if he must know something more, something lying behind the miscellany, something existing, true, real, and more meaningful. So while he suspends his decisions and delicately makes a religious virtue of his search for God, he endeavors to get behind and beneath Scripture, church, commandments, and ordinary believing. The doors are closed, but he finds the keys in the philosophical concepts. Here is the promise of objectivity, existence, and reference. And theism tells us that God is omniscient, omnipotent, omnipresent, omnicompetent, and invisible. It is almost as if, these things being true, now one can trust God, love him, and maybe obey him; but, of course, there is the small matter: Is the conceptual scheme, in turn, really true?

Nowadays there appears to be no one quite qualified to say. For the conceptual ways of getting behind the appearances and the sayings are rather tenuous. Theism is no longer obvious, and, because of difficulties, the contemporary theistic notions are becoming highly specialized. Of course, Christians do learn to use concepts of love, hope, grace, prayer, God, holiness, forgiveness, and many many more in rather workaday ways. Liturgy, prayers, hymns, sermons, the Bible, and other forms of religious language also serve to put such concepts to work upon a wide range of phenomena. The web of language catches up and construes a wide variety of everyday things for us, and with more or less success does a variety of jobs for us. Perhaps this is one reason why being a religious person requires also that one practice that faith; for the practice is also the matter of saying prayers and reading Scripture—in other words, using that faithful language as one's own, thereby keeping the words of faith as the ruling motifs for daily life. Here the Christians indeed do use religious concepts. Here we do not find the words of theistic metaphysics at all. In fact, the only way to get in on theistic metaphysical words is by doing up special theories about God's existence and his nature, which is a very special and a very artificial and contrived thing to do.

In church and home, we do not need an abstract set of concepts at all. Our situation is perhaps comparable to that of the automobile mechanic who repairs cars—generators, ignitions, bearings, engines, and transmissions. Indeed he uses concepts, and quite responsibly. It is a mistake to insist that he is bereft of anything important for the repair of cars if he does not know the atomic weights, molecular structures, and the coefficients of expansion for various materials with which he is working. The point is that in most circumstances the repairman does not need such concepts at all. Just as we learn to use the concepts of "hearing" and "seeing" without correspondingly needing to know the concepts of "sense impression," so the metalworker gets along without the concept of "valence." Because we say that every metal has a coefficient of expansion, a valence, and an atomic weight, we tend to think that the concepts for metals in cars include the chemical concepts of metals. But this is not the case. One need not know anything about atomic weight in order to talk well about automobiles and their pathology. The concepts for small things are not *in* concepts for large things the way atoms are *in* supposedly everything else. This is why the matter of doing philosophy and theology by analysis can also be deceptive, for it often feeds upon the notion that concepts are ingredient the way molecules are in a glass of water, or vitamins are in food—or God is in Christ. But in all the examples, it is clear that using concepts like those for foods, for cars, and for everyday things does not presuppose knowledge of the concepts for vitamins, atomic weights, and other specialist-described ingredients. Likewise, the concepts of theistic metaphysics are not components in most of the concepts of God wrought for us by Scripture, prayers, and liturgy—perhaps, too, by most sermons.

The argument that the meaning of saying "I believe in God the Father, maker of heaven and earth" can only be ascertained by recourse to a theistic metaphysics is a case in point. The notion of a timeless deity who exists anterior to everything else that exists is, obviously enough, an attempt to do justice to both the Creed of the Apostles and to the Genesis narrative. But the argument is invalid, because saying the creed does not suppose that the concepts of God must always include everything that is said about him in the specialist context, any more than speaking of engines supposes knowledge of atomic weights. The mechanic has enough concepts to identify and to repair cars and their parts—other concepts serve other roles and are often used by other people. The able mechanic also "understands" the workings of the automobile in his ordinary concepts. It would be a mistake to say that he needs the concepts of chemistry and physics to get the "true" understanding.

Again, the Creed secures the worshipper's attention, straightens his dispositions, and shakes him loose from worldly and transitory loyalties. If the concept of God works to this effect in that context, that is quite enough. Here there are all kinds of meaning; and it is only a play upon the word *meaning* that makes it seem that the concept of God in the highly abstract and specialized context is more meaningful.

On the contrary. The specialized concepts often mean less rather than more. For such concepts in these abstruse and artificial contexts often have very little work to do. Typically it is only the special metaphysical context that keeps such concepts alive. The irony is that the long-standing academic prejudice about which we are speaking has conditioned the intelligentsia to believe that every use of religious language is *ipso facto* an employment of theistic concepts. The case is no longer argued; it is simply assumed. Thus, many people are made anxious by the decay of metaphysical allegiances, arguing that if these evaporate, then one cannot hope to convert people to the true faith, or then religious language will clearly be meaningless. This is as mistaken as to assume that the concept of iron for the miner depends upon getting the concept of iron also clear in the contexts of chemistry and physics. Even if "iron" should prove to be no longer a viable chemical concept, still "iron" has an established role for miners, ironmongers, manufacturers, and probably even for the chemist when he works around his house. So, too, the concepts of Christian and Jewish faith are not derived from specialist contexts, nor from philosophical or psychological concepts referring to spiritual entities.

The theistic conceptual scheme is not then "in" ordinary religious language at all. But this is not to say that one must therefore think "secularly," as a certain contemporary fashion has it, or that one must revert to a kind of premetaphysical and maybe mythical kind of thinking. The language of prayers, liturgy, and Scripture is by itself neither mythical nor metaphysical, secular nor divine. When put to work in a very responsible and exacting way, the words of prayer, liturgy, and Scripture come to have meaning just as they are. They do not need to be interpreted in order to mean something when they become efficacious for a whole variety of tasks. It is only when they are put to hard and continuing tasks, as they are when we think with them and through them, that we get any kind of conceptual worth at all. Concepts are, after all, chiefly the concentrations of practice and behavior, intent and thought, that give shape and constancy and therefore meaning to our discourse and to our lives.

It is tempting, too, to assume that a theistic scheme is like a code or a table for a game, which we can look up, and by which we fix thereafter the concepts of our religion. Theism is no such code. The truth here is a little hard, for we can only surmise the codes for the meaning of everyday religious concepts out of the conduct of such concepts in religious behavior and literature; and in the last analysis, not even the Bible is so conclusive a reference work that it tells us about every possible misreading. This is said in order to remind us that the meanings of religious words are laden with freight picked up in the religious life. But this does not say that the religious life is theory-free. Just as terms for automobiles in the repairman's vocabulary become laden by the learning that he and countless others have slowly acquired, so too are the special terms of a scientist describing iron and other elements fraught with chemical theory. The words are saturated by their associations within chemical theory, but not by philosophical or other kinds of theories. Therefore, there is a dependence of terms upon theory, and to change the theory often means to change the meaning of the terms; for theories are also one kind of context in which words work, and in which they get and lose their meanings.

Accordingly, we wish to note here that theological terms are not dependent upon philosophical theories, nor even upon the scheme called theism. This does not say that they are "only words," or "atomistic," or "nominalistic," or "relativistic," or without conceptual meaning. The situation is that religious concepts (and specifically Christian concepts, the only ones I have a standing familiarity with) depend upon the somewhat piecemeal outlook and piecemeal theories that bind them together. Creeds, the Bible, prayers, and liturgies call up views of the way people, the world, God, and everyday things are, and they enjoin behavior. There is quite enough theory in these pieces of literature to satisfy one with that kind of hunger. On the other hand, to invoke a philosophical scheme like theism in order to constitute that embedded theory, and to serve as the foundation or the conceptual meaning for all the rest, seems to be as confused an endeavor as to suggest to the automobile mechanic that he get in on chemical valences before he touches the car—or worse, that we ask both the mechanic and the inorganic chemist to get in on a philosophical scheme of reality before they repair a car or do their chemistry.

Atheism and theism are positions generated by mistaking the way Christian and other religious concepts come to mean something. Both of these positions once seemed to have a kind of merit precious to intellectuals. They placed the religious concepts in a kind of scheme where they became systematized and capable of being addressed en masse. A kind of labeling and ordering became possible; and one exulted in being able to reject or to accept a large number at once. But this apparent virtue of homogenizing concepts is sillier in religious matters than it is in science. For the religious life involves, on the conceptual side, a veritable welter of concepts, just as on the behavioral side we have to say that it consists of all kinds of things from prayers to praise, from faith to hope, from patience to obedience, and from loving God to loving one's neighbor. Its concepts are variegated and heterogeneous, but are no poorer for that.

9

Theology and Knowing God

"Now what is theology?" asks John Henry Newman. His answer is plain and unequivocal: "I simply mean the Science of God, or the truths we know about God put into system; just as we have a science of the stars, and call it astronomy, or of the crust of the earth, and call it geology."[1] In another context, Newman says: "Religious doctrine is knowledge, in as full a sense as Newton's doctrine is knowledge. University education without theology is simply unphilosophical. Theology has at least as good a right to claim a place there as astronomy."[2] For a variety of reasons that Newman cites at great length, theology, like other branches of knowledge, "is valuable for what its very presence in us does for us by a sort of 'opus operatum.'"[3] He insists that theology is one of the three subjects developed by "human reason" and has as its subject matter, God. It stands parallel in principle, form, and logic to the physical and social sciences, whose differences with it lie only in their subject matter—nature and man, respectively.[4]

There is something obvious and attractive about a view like Newman's. It needs no explanation, for it accords almost immediately with the ordinary and widespread conceptions of "knowl-

---

[1] All of these remarks are taken from Newman's lectures of 1852, assembled in *On the Scope and Nature of University Education* (London, 1955), pp. 46–47.
[2] Ibid., p. 29.
[3] Ibid., p. 84.
[4] Ibid., p. 190.

edge" and "truth," and with the familiar everyday practices of
teaching and learning. Newman was making the case for theology
in a new university, and he traded on a consensus that was almost
creedal for his academic community. He invoked notions of
"truth," "objectivity," "logic," and "belief" that looked like the
components of a grid of necessary, unambiguous, invarient, and
established fundamental concepts by which everything or anything intellectual could be analyzed, judged, and deemed worthy,
rational, and plainly sensible.

Thus, Newman writes as though God is objective and can
therefore be talked about in the same senses that we write about
stars, the crust of the earth, people, or animals. He appeals to his
university audience on grounds that are plausible and also standard for intellectual practice. Theology is plainly fit for the
university because it can be taught in the same way as most other
subjects. If the religious teachings are true and meaningful in
themselves, then obviously they can be imparted directly and
without difficulty.

Such a view is exceedingly appealing for it accords, in a
superficial way at least, with the affirmation of the First Vatican
Council that God can be known with certainty by the natural light
of human reason. Furthermore, it puts Christian conviction within
the pale of evidence, and it makes it look as if there is a kind of
rational undergirding for the religious life. In short, Newman's
contentions suggest that Christians are not only told to believe in
an authoritative way, but that they are told to believe because
such and such truths do obtain. What obtains is the theology. That
theology tells us about God, and Newman can list dozens of items
about God, all of them ostensibly true predicates, which are
justifying truths for the life of faith. Newman does not deny
revelation or knowing by faith; but it is as though both God's
revelation and the many-sided activity of living faithfully (including the experience, the *agape*, the fellowship, and communion)
are grounded upon a knowledge of God that theology can impart.

Theology as Newman delineates it is often described as a kind of backing for the Christian religion. More than this, the Catholic Church has repeatedly voiced the notion that this backing is reasonable, objective, unequivocal, and even independent of revelation. And there is another kind of ecumenicity that has developed between Christian groups, not least between some Catholics and some Protestants, on this very issue—namely, the view that "a rational approach to theology" is a minimal essential.[5] To an extent that is often baffling to outsiders, the evangelical movements that emphasize the authority of the Bible also want to insist that there is a kind of theological science that support the claims of the Bible to be the truth. A related kind of rationalism develops, too, among the readers of John Calvin. If Calvin is right, a minimal knowledge of God appears to be almost native to honest persons, and even more knowledge of God than that can be surmised from the way the universe is constituted and governed.

No wonder, then, that theology as an enterprise and subject matter is taken with such seriousness. The way of describing theology here promises the very rudiments of rationality, and this to Catholics, Protestants, liberals, and conservatives. Furthermore, to speak as Newman has done is to draw attention to a side of religion that is often forgotten. The Christian faith has often appeared to be an outright superstition and almost a tissue of fable and nonsense. Thus, in the name of theology, Christians have asserted that there are criteria and standards, and that being a Christian is not sheer madness, willfulness, subjectivity, and blind belief. With the talk about miracles, faith, incarnation, creation, judgment, and revelation, it has often seemed that order and discipline, logic and validity, belonged to secular science and not to faithful people and the friends of God. I wish to praise the motives here while reserving the right to criticism.

This rational aspect of theology has never manifested itself as an accident of particular minds, nor has it been an occasional

---

[5] See Walter M. Horton, *Christian Theology: An Ecumenical Approach* (New York, 1955), p. 74. In the instances cited above, the expression *natural theology* is purposely avoided, but *rational theology* might include it.

emphasis of a particular school or a prophetical interpretation. Neither has it looked like an intellectual fashion or a splendid work of a philosophic genius. Instead, it has had a place, if not a role, in the thought world almost since the beginning. Its hold upon us is something like that of logic itself, which did not, as John Locke said, need Aristotle to make us rational. Theology, in the sense we are describing it here, has been like something tacit finally being made explicit, like criteria being disclosed rather than provided. No crisis or particular insight seems to have produced it. Its reception by the most various minds and in differing systems of religiosity otherwise hostile to each other has been argued to be a kind of *prima facie* claim for it.[6] Certainly the very structure of our everyday language, plus the way we use *true, false, objective, rational,* and *real,* make this theological lore almost axiomatic. We can hardly help assuming it without the most exacting scruples.

But this is only if we share rather generously in what one might call the intellectual traditions, not necessarily everything folkish and common. Certainly the Western tradition, going back to Plato and Aristotle, articulates this mode of rationality, including that for religion, most tellingly. All the more reason, then, why most of us who became educated think that theology as a minimal knowledge of God is really but a modicum of intelligence being applied to a facet of human culture that would otherwise be untended and a random growth. Logic and rationality purport to be only formal and a matter of giving a proper shape to inquiry and a discipline to ideas. Nothing substantive is supposedly being proposed if one requires evidence, asks for justification, and seeks for answers. It looks, instead, as if only a necessary rationality is finally being brought to bear upon the Christian faith. Theology is the outcome of that rational and altogether human methodology.

But in our day we have had several challenges directed to this state of affairs. A kind of popular and textbook rendition of one of

---

[6] Newman, op. cit., pp. 51–54.

these challenges is attributed to Søren Kierkegaard and to Karl Barth; for it is alleged that they deny the "facts" by which theology (as the neutral knowledge of God) claims objective justification and propose rather that all knowledge of God comes through special revelation. Then God's revelation alone becomes the backing for religion, and there is no way to criticize or to evaluate revelation itself. For a variety of reasons, I find such an account of Kierkegaard and Barth misleading and wrong. But it is undeniable that both of these thinkers have called into question the notion that there are single and unequivocal concepts of reason, logic, objectivity, and criteria that the intellectualist tradition has invoked. Barth does this by painstakingly tracing the lineaments of the thoughts of the Biblical authors and showing rather conclusively that they do not fit the familiar paradigms. But he does not deny kinds of paradigms or criteria.[7] He does, however, revoke theology of this long-standing fashion in favor of another paradigmatic conception of a churchly and Biblical dogmatics.

Another permutation is attributed to Kierkegaard, who is alleged to have been an anti-rationalist, a subjectivist, and a proponent of faith at the expense of logic and evidence. To a casual reader, Kierkegaard's many books appear to espouse the same beliefs that Newman attributed to Protestantism and Luther: that faith was not an intellectual act; that the object of faith was not true propositions; that the result was not divine knowledge but rather "a feeling, an emotion, an affection, an appetency"; and that "nothing was objective, everything subjective, in doctrine."[8] Once more, we have to admit that Luther and Kierkegaard have a great deal in common, but whether this is another position (as the critics say), one called anti-rational and subjective, revelational and psychological, is a moot point. Kierkegaard actually redid the

---

[7] These points and others are made in greater detail in the essay "Karl Barth and the Logic of Belief," which will appear in a volume by the author on *Logic and the Theologians*.

[8] Newman, op. cit., pp. 16–17.

geography of religious beliefs, and his reflections about faith, logic, and doctrines amount to a new morphological account—an account that criticizes the tradition on what constitutes rationality, the giving of reasons, and even where the line must be drawn between objectivity and subjectivity. Once more, one has to note that Kierkegaard, like Luther, refuses to be judged by the popular standard of rationality; rather is it the case that both of them are questioning that standard itself and noting its irrelevance. A host of other logical and rational criteria is being proposed instead.

For it is not the case that there is an ineluctable and necessary kind of rationality to which we are all beholden. It is precisely that conception of rationality, the notion of a singular and sovereign rationality, that was questioned by Luther and has been more technically and professionally diagnosed in Kierkegaard's *Philosophical Fragments* and *Concluding Unscientific Postscript*. However, repudiating that model of rational theology, phrased for us here by Newman, does not imply irrationality or even theological skepticism. The fact that Wittgenstein and other analytic logicians have made strong remarks about forms of life having an ultimacy has also created the notion that theology is like metaphysics in not being any longer the final court of justification. If forms of life are foundational, then it looks as though fideism is more crucial than theology. So it is that followers of Wittgenstein and Wittgenstein himself are assumed to be of the mind that denies that there is a recognizable kind of knowledge of God and that therefore theology is not truly cognitive, objective, and rational. Oddly enough, Barthians, Kierkegaardians, and Wittgensteinians together look like the opponents of cognitivity and rationality in religion, but only if a certain pattern of rationality is taken to be normative.

It is the argument of these pages that theology is not knowledge of God by analogy with physics and geology. Surely Newman and Christian intellectuals are wrong here. But they are not wrong in insisting that persons can come to know God and that theology has a great deal to do with that. Even theology, however, involves indirect—not direct—communication, and there is no direct reception of that communication, either. The thesis of these pages is that when Christianity is made into something primarily theological and doctrinal, then the nature of faith becomes malformed, as if it were chiefly an act of belief in the doctrine. Subsequently, every person would then be required to understand the theology, and the gist of being a Christian would be a matter of comprehension, just as one might say that being a geologist is a matter of ever deepening and broadening the intellectual grasp.

The effect of much of recent theological reflection, like that of Barth and Kierkegaard, has been to raise doubts about the long-standing conventional metatalk about theology. I have pushed the issues of faith and Christian practice to show that theology has a subservient but crucial role in producing the consciousness of God. The attacks of the philosophers, especially Wittgenstein and other logicians, have also made us see on independent grounds the limits of reasoning in one area after another, and how the harmony between thought and reality, between what is said and what is, is to be found in the rules and structure of the language itself.[9] For there is no single and comprehensive logic, no univocal and necessary kind of reason, the same for all domains. Human reasoning is polymorphic, depending upon the interests and the subject matter, and therefore the "grammars," the "logics," are various. But this does not mean that, in the interest of Christianity, there is no logic and no grammar. Here the critics are wrong. Sometimes, the anxieties of Barth and Kierkegaard (almost like Luther) to clear the air and push the whoring rationalists aside make the diatribe against logic and rules too sweeping. At this

---

[9] Ludwig Wittgenstein, *Zettel*, ed. G. E. M. Anscombe and G. H. von Wright, trans. G. E. M. Anscombe (Oxford, 1967), p. 12e. The passage reads: "Like everything metaphysical the harmony between thought and reality is to be found in the grammar of the language."

point, care and precision must be exercised once more to get justice done. There is a grammar and logic to faith, and theology is part of that.

A further exploration of these issues is assayed in what follows.

I I

A point to remember about "knowing God" is that the concept "knowing" is always context-determined. Thinking about "knowing" is exceedingly difficult, if not nonsensical; for we never just "know." This is why the science of "epistemology," an erstwhile philosophical discipline supposedly about the methods and origin of knowing, proves not to be a science at all. The concept of "knowing" turns out not to be a standard state of mind, nor is it a mode of consciousness or a process. Knowing does not consist in any one thing. This is why we say that "knowing" is context-determined and that the concept of "knowing" is ambiguous, usually because it is susceptible of several meanings, each of which is regularized according to the respective setting. This is also why there is no general epistemology.

Knowing one's ABC's is perhaps something like knowing French. To know ABC's and French bespeaks an aptitude for a large variety of activities, but such knowledge is dispositional, not a state of consciousness. Knowing another's name is different from knowing the person named. In the first instance, I show my knowledge by a referring use of a word; in the second instance, I evince my knowledge of a person, even if I cannot remember his or her name, by citing characteristics, predicting responses, describing propensities, attributing motives, and noting all kinds of other intimate matters. I either know the name or I do not, almost as I know the date of the battle or I do not; but knowing a person calls for understanding, and that one has more likely in degree and never in a single context. One knows a name by remembering it; but one does not remember people and thereby know them, except in a lesser sense.

One knows physics in ways that are different from knowing mathematics. One might have to know mathematics in order to know physics, but, still, knowing numbers and their uses and interpretations is highly conceptual in ways that are distinct from knowing theories and their applications. Perhaps enough has been noted already to see that the highly generalized idea that all knowledge is propositional does not begin to do justice to kinds of knowing. For we cannot quite describe knowing simply as an affair of entertaining propositions. To know a person, or a name, or mathematics is not very significantly described as "knowing," or "entertaining," or "believing" a proposition. Propositions do not quite enter in the clear way that a general epistemology suggests. Knowing is more various.

Knowing a poem or knowing Tolstoy's literature or knowing Aristotle may involve scholarship and all kinds of literary theories and biographical and historical facts; but then again, it may not. There is a way of knowing the Scriptures that requires the capacity to reproduce and to apply its thoughts and to extend the sovereignty of the passions and the ideas therein, and that has little to do with facts and theories. So, too, some people become Aristotelian and Tolstoyan because they know those authors so well. If one knows how to play a game, the contexts there suggest strategies and practices, a sizing up of the opposition, and a wisdom in practice that is a far cry from a geologist's knowing. But think, then, of knowing oneself.[10] The person who is importuned by follies and envy that can never be satisfied is justly said to be without self-knowledge. The person who is careful of his health but negligent of his life is thought a fool, but not simply ignorant. Here a lack of knowledge bespeaks the lack of self-clarification and all kinds of resolutions of will and spirit. The muddy periods, the talkative eloquence in praise of fidelity and other virtues, the confusion between the praise of goodness and

---

[10] Samuel Johnson's remarks on this topic put much of the race into his debt. Note especially the *Rambler* essays, particularly nos. 28, 54, 110, 131, 180, and 206.

the practice—all of these show us how difficult it is to know oneself. Here as in mathematics one typically does not know and mean by this that one has propositions in which to believe![11] Knowing here has an altogether different environment and dissimilar accompaniments.

Now we must think again about knowing God. "Is not the being of God reported to us by testimony, handed down by history, inferred by an inductive process, brought home to us by metaphysical necessity, urged on us by the suggestions of our conscience? It is a truth in the natural order, as well as in the supernatural."[12] Once more, Newman seems to press every analogy and to insist that theology is the purest instance of knowing, the quintessential and embodied example. However, this kind of view blurs the differences between the kinds of knowing that we have been describing. Something of his emphasis must be saved, however, before we go on to further criticism.

A kind of theology surely is taught and widely so. Newman found it necessary to argue the case for teaching what we would call perhaps religious ideas. That issue has been won, and long since, in most countries where Christianity and Judaism are seriously considered. No longer do we believe that such theology is only a projection, an imposition, or an idiosyncratic expression of a group or a person. Under the name of theology many things masquerade. "Theology is a science, but at the same time, how many sciences!" says Pascal.[13] Under the rubrics of scholarly and scientific studies of religion, a kind of formalizing of the language of faith has taken place. A result is that under theology (and/or religious studies) we now study a variety of the religious phenom-

---

[11] "But you surely don't believe a mathematical proposition." This is cited for discussion by Wittgenstein in *Remarks on the Foundations of Mathematics*, trans. G. E. M. Anscombe (New York, 1956), p. 33e.

[12] Newman, op. cit., p. 14.

[13] Blaise Pascal, *Pensées* (Montreal, 1944), aphorism no. 115, p. 112. "La theologie est une science, mais en même temps combien est-ce de sciences!" The translation is my own.

ena, all in the "about" mood. So we study the concepts of "love," "faith," "grace," "God," and numerous others, plus historical and Biblical fields, too.

Theology includes both studies in the "about" mood (a language *about* the things of faith) and the language of faith itself.[14] What so many persons mistakenly have come to believe is that a scientificlike language in the "about" mood is the only language that is logical, evidential, objective, and rational. The other language is metaphorical, symbolic, figurative, and even emotive. Also, most of us have come to believe that the best knowledge we have is in the erstwhile disinterested and "about" mood. That, however, is plainly wrong. As I have just noted, there is no single logic and context for "knowing." There is no one and sure way to be objective—i.e., to address matters of fact and speak about what is. Instead, the person who speaks in the "of" mood, whose life is already formed by searching for God with all of his or her heart, also finds a considerable language of faith already designed for seekers. That language does not simply express a way of life, but it, too, becomes extended into a language about everything else in the world. It is a language of *connaître* rather than *savoir*.

What I have said about the word *knowledge*—namely, that it is context-determined and hence is used for a variety of conceptual purposes—must also be said about *objective, true,* and even *real*. Thus, when someone says: "What I want to know is whether theology is 'objective' and not just a party line," the question does not permit the plain and unequivocal answer that is often being sought. The better part of wisdom is not to answer the question directly; for either *yes* or *no* tends to buttress the vulgar academic prejudice that lurks in the question. A prejudice is, among other things, an idea about which one refuses to think. And it is an academic and hence a confoundedly difficult prejudice to eradicate—namely, that *objective, real, true, logical, rational,* and other words of this extensive criteriological sort are manifest in

---

[14] Note Chapter 4, "Scientific Language and the Language of Religion."

meaning, unvariegated in use, simple to understand, and plainly rudimentary and underived in import. Though we use them in every context, and though we all are endowed with sufficient capacity to use some of them in telling ways, they are still not transcendentals and context-free. The fact is that they are used in several contexts, and they become context-dependent. So we have to be clear about the specifics in each case. *Rational, objective, true, real,* etc., are always "in respect to so and so"; and then the expressions make sense and engage a subject matter and a thinker.

What the medieval tradition and then Kant in the eighteenth century made of such concepts is rather starkly described in the doctrines about transcendentals. Kant not only thought that there were transcendentals, but philosophy itself became the science not of the transcendent God or a transcendent reality beyond all experience, but of the transcendentals. If we place our discussion in Kant's context, we might say that philosophy was for him the science about ideas and concepts that were implied in and necessary to an experience but were not products thereof. They transcended ordinary ideas and were described as *a priori*—i.e., independent of empirical experience. Once more, the view was that the criteriological words were "trans" (across) all fields and interests and were truly, as the medievals called them, "transcendentalia." Logic and pure rationality invoked such concepts and gave order and validity to everything else we thought and experienced. My argument, however, is that there is no way to give sense to such a thesis. I am not arguing an alternative as much as I am invoking the criteria in other contexts.

Nonetheless, it is a downright prejudice to believe that "knowledge" has a singular grammar or logic.[15] Or that logic has a

---

[15] Once more I am using the word *grammar* in Wittgenstein's sense. He says early in his use of the term (probably in 1929): "Philosophy as custodian of grammar can in fact grasp the essence of the world, only not in the propositions of language, but in rules for this language which exclude nonsensical combinations of signs" (*Philosophical Remarks*, ed. Rush Rhees, trans. Raymond Hargreaves and Roger White [Oxford, 1975], p. 85). See also *Philosophical Investigations*, trans. G. E. M. Anscombe (Oxford, 1953), p. 116e: " 'Essence' is expressed by grammar."

peculiar depth and universal significance and somehow explores and delimits the nature of everything, theology included. There is both an attractiveness and an obscurity lurking in these very dignified concepts and domains. To escape the obscurity is also to escape the glitter and charm. But the escape is easy. It involves an attitudinal change and a willingness to consider the context in which one is raising the questions. Therefore, the questions to which I alluded earlier, about whether theology is an objective science, propositional and true, have no across-the-board answer. Instead one has to show the interlocuter that *objective* in this instance must mean the opposite of a whim or a fancy. If so, then theology (at least the language of faith) about God and, for example, his making of the world is not an invention of the speaker—it is used referringly and is not an index to the faith of the speaker and not a clue to an individual's consciousness. On the other hand, it is not fiction or poetry either, for theology does not require that we be prepared for a kind of feigning of character and a simulation of events. Its normal tone of address is complete seriousness and primitive honesty. These again are suggested by its very grammar.

Two things can be said, then, about theology and the knowledge of God. There is a branch of theology, a kind of religious study, that is objective and formally describable by the same range of canons that we use for most observational knowledge. Thus theology can be the study of concepts used in religious and Christian contexts. (The theology called "Lundensian" and exemplified by Nygren's *Agape and Eros* and several of the works of Aulen are conceptual studies like that.) Theology can then share the same criteria of objectivity, evidence, and probative value that we would have in philosophy, law, and politics, where conceptual studies abound. But theology might and does also include the study of the rationale for sacraments, the shape and content of doctrines, similarities and differences, and origin and history, and it also shares features of certain historical disciplines. Under theology we might also have inquiries that are sociological, political, and legal, again sharing criteria, scope, and methods with other intellectual practices.

But this kind of theology is not quite about God—it is about ideas, institutions, sacraments, persons, thinkers, morals, and the rest. On the other hand, there is the language of faith itself, and that can be studied, too. Here, however, a different set of conditions obtain. The grammar is altogether different. Such a language requires a different context and another setting before even its sense is manifest. The language of faith brings us much closer to the actual knowledge of God. Notwithstanding, that language of faith still does not impart the knowledge of God directly. The Apostle says: "Give thanks to the Father, who has qualified us to share in the inheritance of the saints in light" (Col. 1:12). There is a strong sense in which the Christian teacher, the theologian, dares to become a kind of guardian of such a remark and many more like it. For the essence of Christian teaching is available, not just in the commands and the assertions themselves, but in the rules and grammar of this language. These rules require that we speak of God as Father; that we be among those qualified in a stupendous manifold of ways; that we be contrite, repentant, hopeful, and zealous; and that we be enabled to distinguish saints from the ungodly, the light from darkness. After a bit, even a remark like this one does not get its sense only from other sentences that surround it, but also from the mode of life in which it is natural and even obvious, and from the persons and situation to whom and to which it is addressed. The grammar involves more than words. How profound words are understood is not told by more words alone.

The language of faith is found paradigmatically chiefly in the Christian Scriptures and the liturgy, but also in less exalted forms in the mouths of saints and believers through human history. That language can be assimilated by acts of obedience and a simple kind of following. There seems to be no general reason to exempt anyone from doing and feeling and thinking as it says. At least, there is no lofty general kind of pronouncement that suggests attenuating circumstances and a lessening of the demand. When Albert Schweitzer said that most of the stern remarks of Jesus were posited on the notion of his immediate return to the human scene, Schweitzer was making a grammatical and typically theological remark in the modern sense. His comment placed much of the New Testament in a new context, albeit mistakenly, and changed the import of much of what Jesus had said.[16]

People become Christian by obeying the first-person language of the Bible and making themselves at home in it. One could surely be glad in such circumstances not to be a great theologian, for one might too easily mistake this for being a good Christian. Theologians are prone to read the Bible and to think with a special interest. So, too, do some scholars who read the Bible as great literature and then miss most of what it is about. If one reads the Bible as a theologian, one might add nothing but spiritual pride to pedantry and conceit, already endemic among the learned. Theology as grammar is surely no shortcut to God. In matters of faith and knowing God, it certainly obtains that every acquisition in the direction of certainty is valuable in proportion to the difficulty employed in its attainment.

Theology, in the wide sense alluded to, is a technical and truly professional enterprise. But in most of what passes as theological study, one never even approximates the essence of Christianity, let

---

[16] The notion that many of the ethical demands of Jesus are eschatological is not quite a hypothesis. Evidence does not quite settle the matter, nor refute it either. Like most "grammatical" remarks, a certain kind of fittingness and meaning, a logical drift of the totality, has to bear one out. The persons who can speak to this have to be qualified by an acquaintanceship at firsthand with the mode of judging, sizing up, thinking, evaluating, etc., to which the language itself is an intimate and "internal" party. The language "of" faith, like that "of" art, taste, conscience, etc., is not about thinking and evaluating—it is the instances of these capacities. Therefore, the conclusion as to what is the grammar is not a hypothetical and contingent judgment; instead, it is a part of the understanding itself. Therefore, quarrels here are quite different from mere points of view, positions, etc. Schweitzer is wrong, for example, because he did not understand the sayings of Jesus and how they were embedded in a radically different way of life. He read them as if they were "Goethe-like," "ethical," and "humanistic."

alone the knowledge of God. Getting to know the grammar of
faith is another matter altogether. Here the skills are also typically
indigenous to the educated, plus there is one other factor: a
firsthand acquaintance with the form of life that makes a person a
Christian. Even without the latter, the logic and permanent shape
of Christianity sometimes begin to shine through the teachings,
the modes of life, and the churchly liturgy and practices. At least
it is conceivable that a theologian can describe a lot of what he or
she might not intimately share. The prospect of seeing the oddness
of a morphology of ideas, however, is so difficult under the best of
conditions that it is unlikely that someone unsympathetic would
see it. But one can not pontificate here. Nietzsche's aversion to
Christianity was so profound and so detailed that his pages outline
a faith in Jesus that is worthy of offense. For this reason, his work
helps us to see how blessed someone is who is not offended by
Jesus. Nietzsche understood but was antipathetic. Voltaire's contention that Pascal's account of Christianity is misanthropic suggests that both Voltaire and Pascal had seen the logic of faith
correctly. In one sense, both had the grammar straight—one so
that he could accept it, the other so that he could at least reject the
right thing.

Such a straightening of thought is about all that theology as
grammar can finally do; but from one standpoint it is quite
enough. It tells us what the essence of the matter is, and that can
be straightforward, realistic, and true, and not just an opinion.
Isn't this all the nearer to faith any third-person account can bring
us?

Thus far, I have noted that there is a kind of theological study
that shares the logic of the history of ideas, of sociology, and of
other empirical studies. These subjects, though amenable to popular pedagogy, are not likely to tell one what and who God is. But
another use of the word *theology*—namely, as a grammar or
logic—is certainly a bit closer to that end. By and large, however,
theology is an accounting of how the concepts, including the
concept of "God," hang together. One can get the drift of things

thereby, and that is not to be made lightly of. But knowing the grammar because of a competence in the language of faith itself is another and profoundly different accomplishment. Perhaps this is like knowing a surface grammar, as a child learns a rule, and a depth grammar, where you cannot state the rule any longer but your conduct bears out the rule at every juncture.

I I I

It is tempting to think that we can put the truth of Christianity into everybody's heads by a pedagogical device or by ever revising the concepts. We are led very quickly to the thought that we fail to provide knowledge of divine reality for the same reason that the atomists of ancient time failed to give us analytical chemistry. The concepts of Democritus, Leucippus, and Lucretius were anagogical instead of empirical, and their conceptual nets are positively crude compared to modern physics and chemistry. Therefore, we are prone to think that the difficulty is that divine realities are too refined for the crudities of everyday talk and even for the loose forms of Biblical discourse, and that we need a more refined notational system to state what is what about God.

Once we have accepted the notion that theology is knowledge by analogy with other sciences, then we are subject also to continually revising the conceptual schemes that make up our knowledge—except that in theology, as in philosophy, the guiding theme tends to be that we must have new theologies in order to state the meanings. Therefore, we get theologies that are new conceptual systems, designed around some aspects of modern life and learning that are especially taxing and suggestive. For example, because the conceptual distinction between the organic and the inorganic appeared less clear in certain respects than it once had, it became feasible to propose a metaphysical hypothesis called "emergent evolution." That in turn suggested a spectacle of a universe subject to a blind and inarticulate purposiveness, pushing its way upward and onward towards an ever-increasing complexity and eventually even a combination of determinate types capable of genuine spontaneity.[17] If one were looking for a new way to locate the concept "God," one might find it here. All of this invites the notion of spirit and spirituality, almost as if a nisus were incumbent in material things. More than this, it is easy to conceive of nature abiding a *conatus*, a kind of effort or impulse analogous to human effort but infinitely more powerful and efficacious. This, then, is Spirit or God. By a kind of intellectual sleight of hand, this new rendition of the concept of God, drawn from biological philosophy, begins to look like a better way to state the meaning of the concept "God." The older notions of God as person and creator sound outworn and a little antique and metaphorical compared to thinking about God as a "force" and as a power in nature that makes for newer forms of life. Therewithal, the newer theological formulations are said to be the same in "meaning" as the older theological notions, except that the newer are less figurative and mythical, and, of course, more literal.

One need not choose bizarre examples in order to illustrate this inclination to keep theology intellectually responsible. A certain number of people are persuaded that science has brought rationality to maturity, and hence that there is a higher degree of general enlightenment and a better understanding of our world now than earlier ages manifested. It is easy to surmise that early ages were more infantile and that we are more adult. But surely this is, again, that odd chronological prejudice showing itself. It certainly is a bit of fanciful rubbish, and a metaphor besides, to believe that the whole race had an infancy or that mankind once was doomed in toto to being lesser than we, because of being born

---

[17] Examples here are legion. The pages of Bergson's *Creative Evolution* are suggestive, but more can be seen in Teilhard de Chardin's books and by those who think that we must adopt scientific methods in all that we do and say. Supposedly a scientific age requires that we treat even moral and religious issues in that way. An example here is G. Burniston Brown, *Science, Its Method and Its Philosophy* (London, 1950).

earlier. Is it not simply absurd to think that there can be only one standard for all disciplines and that anything not treated either scientifically, or what we are prone to rephrase as "rationally," is therefore less perfect? Obviously, one can be infantile in religious faith as opposed to being adult and mature, but this difference is something that is best taught by the religious life itself.

It is easy, too, to believe that a later kind of learning, perhaps a science or a bit of technical scholarship or a newer theological view, is saying clearly and more adequately what earlier thinkers were fumbling for all along. In this context, it is plausible to posit the notion that the earlier and the later both "meant" the same thing; or that anything once believed and said can now be more accurately expressed in the newer concepts and terms. So when we mark off the technical theology (like that evolutionary view I alluded to) from the everyday talk of Scripture (the language of faith), it is assumed that we have a better grade of accuracy and a distinction in intellectual level, rather than a shift in subject matter. Whatever else these theological schemes are, they are not the bedrock of Christian beliefs. Theological systems as they have proliferated are not improvements that have a universal application; instead they are, at best, a different kind of investigation, maybe an outright invention, in which some people spend their time and talents, to be considered independently of what other people are believing and doing.

Theological inventions, like philosophical schemes, are almost endless in number. Most of them are dependent upon concepts derived from other fields. Thus we have God identified as a "force," a principle of "concretion," a law of the universe, a "function," a subjective fiction, a projection, the absolute, the infinite, the unlimited—in fact, in almost any way but in the manner of the Scriptures. The Biblical accounting in a language of faith is then said to be given its more rational undergirding and literal meaning. All of that supposes, however, that there is a uniquely fundamental and rich way to know, rather than varieties of things to know and appropriate ways to know them. The syntax and notational system of the invented theological systems is not a development of the ordinary language of faith. There are, indeed, sometimes connections, or otherwise theology in the technical forms would barely exist. Here again, we are not speaking of genuinely scholarly enterprises and scientific studies of religions (which pass as "theology"), but principally of theologies as new conceptual and notational systems in which the nature and existence of God is being redescribed so that one can be said to have knowledge of him. Even these latter systems could only be formulated at all if issues were raised and queries promulgated outside of these systems themselves.

In contrast, the language of faith is kept alive and in the edifying use of the Scriptures usually in the worship services of the churches. Most sermons once had to be confined by practice and canon law to keeping that language natural and alive for the Christian congregations. In addition, the sermon extended that language to circumstances and persons not covered by the written and formalized discourse. Orthodoxy in theology is never capable of much more refined definition than that supposed by the somewhat loose consensus of the faithful. Like any natural language, the meaningfulness and liveliness of the discourse "of" faith (rather than the language *about* it) is attributable to many whom one will never see, hear, or speak to. That language of faith, as with ordinary everyday talk, is not charted and plotted for users; instead, one gets it by informal means from the context and from all the ways of being a Christian. It grows with compassion, self-contrition, dismay, grief, unexpected joy, terrifying anxieties, sermons about God, fear of failure and punishment, and in a host of other conditions that occur in an ecology that is uncompromising and natural. No wonder, then, that expressions and circumlocutions soon are in the air, and they flow from the natural way of sizing up one's life, whether St. Paul's, Luther's, yours, or mine. The point is that the language of faith is not an artificial and contrived tongue. People speak in this way and in conjunction with Apostles, saints, and the proposers of law and gospel. *Faith, hope, grace,* and other words become internal to one's life and its vicissitudes. Fairly soon, that language of faith is extended to all of one's planning, judging, wishing, and even the remembrance of things past. Judgments are formed and ideas are formulated as to what life is all about. Knowing God is then not so much a matter of having observational knowledge about, or conceptual mastery of, him, though the latter can be there, too; rather, it has very much to do with a profound qualification of the life that believers lead and to which the language of faith has an untold number of internal relations.

The difficulty with the technical and artificial theologies is that they all sooner or later propose a special vocabulary. The sense that they then have depends on the amount of work that one can get the terms to do. But philosophies, and lately the theologies, can get such special terms to do no more work than their surroundings themselves provide. This is why each system seems to work as one reads it, but the next one does equally well. Skepticism ensues, for there is no outside domain, no context, in which such special expressions have a genuine and useful role. Hence, what one might call the grammar is really missing. There is no way to determine the meaning and sense of the proposed language other than by judging the work done by the expression in the discourse proposing it. This is as much as to say that the discourse is meaningless; furthermore, this explains that terrible scandal of modern theologies, where everything counts equally and skepticism reigns supreme. There is no outside court of appeals.

Once more, one must turn to the language of faith and think about its province. It has no technical vocabulary; rather, it has an ordinary range of words used in very particular ways. This is why *hope* is indeed an ordinary word in almost everyone's life; but the Christian meaning comes from the way that term is now bound up with God, on the one hand, and with a world and an individual, on the other. It is only within these accounts that the word *hope* becomes a distinctive Christian concept and means anything at all. But more importantly, perhaps, being hopeful is not without a grammar that is also public. For like other words that became Christian concepts (*love, belief, grace, peace*, etc.), the point is that it would make no sense to say that a person understands these without there being an exemplification of them. The very logic of the expressions suggests that one must become hopeful, loving, kind, merciful, and the rest. Besides, all these concepts propose a way and are the very terms in which one thinks now of other people and the world and also of oneself. That would not occur if there were no language of faith. Significant theology is a good part of that language of faith. Then, too, we can understand why sharing the logic and grammar means that we will surely share judgments with others—in the Christian sense, with the community of the Blessed. This informal consensus is the heart of orthodoxy.

I V

What, then, about knowing God? We have been crisscrossing the terrain of theology, and it has proved to be very rough country indeed. Partly because religious nurture is so important, it has many counterfeits. All of them have interest, even if little intellectual merit is detected. But now I wish to consider another specific issue entailed by the issue of whether God can be known.

We are tempted to think that God may be an object, though a very different one from other objects. That is part of what is meant by saying he is objective. But this does not get us very far. With objects we have names, and the meaning of names is tied up with the criteria for objects. "That," we say, "is what I mean by a rabbit." The word *rabbit* makes sense for us because we can look at an animal with long ears, a bushy tail, etc., and say: "What is that?" But with God it makes no sense to ask: "What is that?", for we do not have access to him as an object such that we can then go on to give him a name. This objection holds also for those discussions which say, "that force," "that tendency," and then go on: "this we call God." *Force* and *tendency* already get their meanings from another series of criteria, and the latter cannot properly be extended further. Perhaps we have the criteria for *force* in a certain range of circumstances, but not for *God* in the same range.

God is not a proper name, either. We cannot say, "Who is that?" and get the answer, "God." But there are ways to give names to people by pointing to them—we might initially see them as objects, then as people. One cannot do that with God. Once more, this is to say a great deal about the grammar of the expression *God*. Clearly, *God* is not a name but a concept.[18] We learn about that concept in a long story that begins with the origins of the Hebrews and continues through their adventures and trials over many centuries. Thus, a narrative provides a kind of context, and, accordingly, a certain interest we call theological is centered upon narration and all that it entails. But this has been overstressed, for narrations are also our only access to that unforgettable Natasha in Dostoevsky's *The Insulted and Injured,* and to Father Zossima in *The Brothers Karamazov.* The differences are numerous. The most obvious is that the story of the Jews and the subsequent story of Jesus are not told for their own sake. Instead, those stories are linked up with worship and the quality of one's life. Reverence, shame, renewal of one's life, and certain qualities of devotion—these and more give the worship of God some context. More than that, the entire world is brought into the stories of Jesus and of the Jews such that my world and your world, as we read, is also being referred to God and things eternal. The use of the word *God* is thereby being taught to us, and this makes those stories quite different from even the most serious fiction. *God* becomes a concept, not just a name; for he is more like a Mighty Ruler, a King of Kings, Almighty and Everlasting, than he is like King George the Fifth. He is King and kingly, not Zossima or Natasha.

Theology in this context is being learned. For after a while we

---

[18] Kierkegaard's "Johannes Climacus" argues this very forcefully in the *Philosophical Fragments.*

know how to use the word *God* in responsible and patterned ways. A way of speaking is born in us, and with it comes also a way of thinking. It is hard to say which comes first, for the worship and obeisance sustain the thoughts, and the thoughts engender, in turn, the worship. Theology is a name for what is often that tacit awareness of when and how to use the word *God*. That again is what I mean by having the grammar, the rules. They frame for us as much of the essence as we can ever command.

In a very definitive sense, then, there is no such thing as having observational knowledge about God. Even if one chose a transcendent mode of existence, one could not do research on God. There is no investigatory technique, by analogy with most sciences, for finding the facts about God, and theology is surely not a superscience to get at the divine essence. This is why we do not, properly speaking, know God by analogy with knowing geology and astronomy. Right here, then, we have to draw a limit on what it means to know God.

The Bible, the prayer books, the public liturgy, the confessions—these and more are, if they have not been endlessly tampered with and made agreeable to passing whims of the age, the formats within which the knowledge of God is brought to definition. Concepts and ideas are formulated within these matrices, but they are only valid and reliable as religious and Christian ideas if they cause the person to worship God. This is what we mean by getting to know God—namely, that those who know him are those who worship him in spirit and truth. Obviously enough, one's theology also is continually being changed and even enlarged. But theology is not relative, radically contingent, or an each-to-his-own proposition. And some change does not mean that change is the rule of the Christian game, too.

On the contrary, our concepts of "God," the "world," our duties, and how we should think of our lives are embedded in a tradition. That tradition is so rich and many-sided that few of us can ever outlive its contents. We may start with Adam and Eve and God "in the cool of the evening"; but we will soon go on to a

God "who watches over Israel, who neither slumbers nor sleeps."
Soon "God" is "in Christ," too; he is "forgiving" and "merciful,"
but also a terrifying "Judge." "God" can claim all the vengeance,
assert sovereignty over the whole world, demand obedience,
condemn sinners, love the world, and be an abiding presence.
Therefore, there are a host of ways open to us to learn to know
him. Theology tells us what can be said about him, and surely this
permits a chastened and divinely taught intelligence to improvise
slightly. The Scriptures themselves bring us from *Genesis* through
the prophets and show how the tradition both limits and also
empowers those who live in it to attain unheard-of considerations.
The Divine life is charted only in part. Once more, the Scripture
is an antecedent to our faithful lives, as faithful lives were, for
those authors, an antecedent to the Scriptures. This reciprocity is
no license for wild speculation, but it is a clue to the profound
freedom open to lives that unfold in the knowledge of God. What
God is, then, can never be answered for those who read and run.
"Tell me 'how' you seek and I will tell you 'what' you are
seeking," says Wittgenstein.[19] "If with all your heart, ye truly seek
me, ye shall ever surely find me"; that is reported in Scripture as a
saying of the Lord. Knowing God, then, is a matter of coming to
know him in prayer, worship, praise, and much else that makes up
the religious life. Theology, now thinking of it in the grammatical
sense, is not a substitute for worship; and it certainly is not a lofty
and sophisticated way to acknowledge God in contrast to the
vulgar modes of belief and submissive respect. It does not substitute new concepts for those in the story, for that again is no
improvement but is invariably a radically different replacement.
One might say that a new concept usually changes the entire
grammar. Theology is a name, then, for the ruled way, the correct
way, of speaking about and worshipping God. Like grammar in
more mundane instances of everyday speech, theology is both all

---

[19] *Philosophical Grammar,* ed. R. Rhees, trans. Anthony Kenny (Oxford, 1974),
p. 370. In the *Philosophical Remarks,* Wittgenstein says: "Or you might say, a
question 'denotes' a method of searching" (p. 77).

that we have—namely, knowing what is right to say—and also the way one secures the identity of God. So we do not know the true God or know God truly by a simple use of the word *God*. The true God is known only when his identity is established in a tradition and by a ruled practice of language and worship. This is what the grammar, the theology, provides.

V

I have been asserting that "God" is a concept. Obviously, I am not asserting that God is a concept, but only that the word *God* is a kind of accounting, a descriptive and predictable term, and not a name. Therefore, it is very important to say that *God* is used wrongly if used for the moon, the sun, a force in nature, or for objects, idols, and totems. For one thing, if *God* were a proper name, there could be little quarreling that would make any sense; for naming can go on pretty well as one pleases. A name is bestowed and that is all there is to it. But this is what has happened in the modern world when the multiplication of theologies has led to many "Gods." Where no one shares the grammar of God, then a whole set of problems goes dead. If God is a name and theology begins with whatever one happens to name as God, then theologies can no longer mean the same thing and even differ to the extent of contradicting one another. One of the disheartening features of modern theologies is that they have lost their argumentative force in respect to one another. Mostly they pass by without engaging our concerns for truth and falsity, and they live only so long as a fashion or enthusiasm prevails.

We can think of a concept in another context. If I call a man by his name, James, then that word designates "that" person. But if he is Doctor (or president, king, or general), then we have a predicable term for him, too. He either is or isn't what we say in our description. *God* is a descriptive expression and means Holy, Creator, Sustainer, Father of mankind, etc.[20] Therefore, there is a

---

[20] Thomas Aquinas saw, like Kierkegaard, that "God" is a concept. This meant for him that a description went with the term.

way in which the word *God* comes to mean a great deal for those who are nurtured in the Hebrew-Christian tradition. After a while, one learns who and what that God is, but only by training and exposure. The grammar makes it all manifest. This is why we say again that "God" is a concept; for to understand the term is to be empowered to think something definite, to be enabled to use the word *God* in a guarded and responsible sense, and even to disagree with someone who called his or her money, or lover, or an object, "God." Contradictions can arise, and disagreements can appeal to a certain rationale given with the term.

Right here, though, the temptation is to think that one can get beneath or behind one's tradition and justify it. We are prone to think that there are many traditions and hence the possibility of many "Gods," each with its own starting point and its own grammar. Therefore, we would like to believe that there is a more natural and a less historical starting point, a logically necessary way to understand *God*, that would undergird the practice and show us that it is correct. We want a criterion for the correctness independent of the tradition in which the concept comes to exist for us. We want a metaphysical or a logical surety in which to ground Christian beliefs.

Once more, we are back to the point where we began. We are easily seduced into the notion that there are ways to get at the meaning of concepts (almost any of them) that are better than the obvious ones of training, acculturation, scriptural lore, and the rest. We dislike the notion that we learn logic while and when we speak. It seems more rational and more deeply responsible to think that logic is a science of all possible languages, a set of rules for all other rules, and the ultimate court of appeal.

There are very sophisticated ways of exploiting our uneasiness in these matters. Two avenues have been attractive, one via the exploitation of purely logical considerations, the other via some rather variegated attempts to identify our knowledge of other concepts with the knowledge of God. These two I will allow to coalesce, but only because I am showing how easy it is to forsake the religious context when thinking about God. A quotation from a Polish logician will illustrate how logic itself gives an occasion for a passionate reflection about "God":

> As a conclusion to these remarks, I should like to sketch a picture connected with the deepest intuitive feelings I always get about logistic. This picture perhaps throws more light than any discursive exposition would on the real foundations from which this science grows. . . . Whenever I am occupied even with the tiniest logistical problem, e.g., trying to find the shortest axiom of the implicational calculus, I have the impression that I am confronted with a mighty construction, of indescribable complexity and immeasurable rigidity. This construction has the effect upon one of a concrete tangible object, fashioned from the hardest of materials, a hundred times stronger than concrete and steel. I cannot change anything in it; by intense labour I merely find in it ever new details, and attain unshakeable and eternal truths. Where and what is this ideal construction? A Catholic philosopher would say: it is in God, it is God's thought.[21]

No wonder that we are tempted to think that the finer and more abstract distinctions are truer, more solid, and somehow more definitive. This is what prevails with us when the more primitive religious language-game, the story of the Jews, their trials, their fortunes, the story of Jesus' birth, life, and death, and the relation of these things to our lives seem to need justification. We are no longer content with the thought that we ought to revise our lives and that doubting is wrong, even sinful. Wittgenstein says something about this:

> It is the same when one tries to define the concept of a material object in terms of "what is really seen." What we have rather to do is to "accept" the everyday language-game, and to note "false" accounts of the matter "as" false. The primitive language-game which children are taught needs no justification; attempts at justification need to be rejected.[22]

All of that goes against the grain, not least if we are very

---

[21] J. Lukasiewicz, "W obronie Logistyki," in *Z zagadnien logiki i filozofii* (Warsaw, 1961). This quotation is translated by Peter Geach and appears in *A Wittgenstein Workbook*, by Christopher Coope, Peter Geach, Timothy Potts, and Roger White (Oxford, 1970), p. 22.

[22] *Philosophical Investigations*, Part II, p. 200e.

sophisticated. The logician who has seen the hardness and necessity of logical details is prone to make a conceptual stipulation—namely, that knowledge of God is not knowledge until it becomes like the logical truths, that knowledge of the Everlasting God must be at least as rational as those "unshakeable and eternal truths" of which Lukasiewicz and other logicians like Leibniz spoke. The German philosopher Hegel, though so different in outlook on most matters from those we now call logicians, was also so enamored with pure thought that the same discussion passes muster as being both metaphysical and logical. These necessities of pure thought are, for him, also the great truths of fact. And all disciplines and topics suffer a vagueness until they are brought to definiteness; and the rule is "from vagueness to definiteness," whereby almost everything can then be brought into a logical embrace. It is as if logic alone is the necessary grasp of reality.[23] Hegel even dares to find in logic the reason why Jesus Christ "must" come into the world by a genuine historical incarnation.[24] Once more, we encounter the tendency to substitute the logical context for the religious because it is more fundamental. It is as if logicians are subject to a great temptation to analyze and to deduce empirical subject matter, theological truths, metaphysics, and, lately, arithmetic and geometry by means of concepts that belong chiefly to logic.[25]

---

[23] The references here are to Hegel's lesser logic, translated with prolegomena by W. Wallace as *The Logic of Hegel* (Oxford, 1892). See especially Chapter 11.

[24] The references appropriate here are primarily to Hegel's *Philosophy of Religion*, 3 vols. But the point is that every religion can be best understood by its "conception"; and then, according to Hegel, the conception of God in Jesus Christ is best fulfilled in "Absolute Religion," which appears to be Christianity, but now logically restated and purified.

[25] Bertrand Russell said explicitly that "mathematical logic" was not mathematical because it used algebraic signs instead of ordinary prose; instead, it deduced mathematical concepts from those of logic. See "The Philosophical Implications of Mathematical Logic" (1911), included in Bertrand Russell, *Essays in Analysis*, ed. Douglas Lackey (New York, 1973), p. 284. Wittgenstein, though much indebted to Russell, criticized this "deduction." Typical is his question: "And why do we accept the one in place of the other? On grounds of 'logic'?" (*Remarks on the Foundation of Mathematics*, p. 90e). Note also *The Philosophical Grammar*, pp. 344 ff., where another criticism is explored.

So we return to the point noted earlier that the attractiveness of logic is that it provides a standpoint, a firm one, supposedly an inviolate one, by which we can get at and describe plain language from the outside. Not only that, but logic gives the illusion of a penetration deeper than that of theology—or let us say, the language of faith—itself. It also looks as though anything said in arithmetic and geometry is said better in mathematical logic; and the power of logic, Aristotelian and its later developments, has suggested something analogous for theology, too.

Thus, Josiah Royce offers us in his book *The Conception of God*[26] a "philosophical discussion" about the divine idea as a "demonstrable reality." The thrust of his pages is to admit skepticism, which has put him out of sympathy with "many of what seems to me the unessential accidents of religious tradition as represented in the historical faith," but then to go on by a very subtle logical refraction to prove that "God is known as thought fulfilled." The result is that Royce can say: "I am certainly disposed to insist that what the faith of our fathers has genuinely meant by God, is, despite all the blindness and all the unessential accidents of religious tradition, identical with the inevitable outcome of a reflective philosophy."[27]

A medieval tradition would have it that knowing God is like knowing *summum bonum, verum, pulchrum*, the superb degree of goodness, truth and beauty. "God," then, is identified by concepts that all of us find essential in daily life, and the knowledge of God is like an extrapolation from something familiar that provides the major predicates in our speech. Even more subtle and perspicacious is the remarkable exploitation of categories that has gone on in western thought. Perhaps most of us now take this for granted, but the intellectual effort, when thought about disinterestedly, is awesome and confounding. In any case, once we are struck with the notion that thinking has limits and

---

[26] Josiah Royce, *The Conception of God* (New York, 1898).
[27] The quotations are from *The Conception of God*, pp. 45–50.

that categories state them for us, we are in for a variety of taxing meditations. The absolute and the relative, the finite and the infinite, the necessary and the possible, and the temporal and the eternal are among the pairs that are alluring. The portent is that these categorizations actually divide the world into one or the other, and that they are not invented but are, rather, the deepest and most fundamental predicates of the way things are. Aristotle apparently thought that, and most of us are prone to follow him. It is easy to use this category language to give yet another conceptual context to the concept of God. Then God becomes absolute, infinite, eternal, and necessary. Instead of God being identified by the stories of the Old and New Testaments, we now have him made legible by connection with a neutral category system, ostensibly necessary to all of mankind. The difficulty is a slight one—namely, that categories must be assumed to be the predicates of being itself. Without that metaphysical premise, the whole endeavor becomes a mere shuffling of ideas. I shall not pause to criticize this endeavor, for that belongs to another lengthy inquiry.

V I

We are back to the issue once more of what the knowledge of God actually is. Knowing God is not a matter of sharing an observational knowledge. Instead, it is an immediate, nonobservational knowledge. But the immediate kind of knowing here is, as Kierkegaard said of faith, "after reflection." The grammatical knowledge of God, almost a dialectical and conceptual knowledge of God, plus the historical knowledge of Jesus, are but part of the prolegomenon to knowing God. The prolegomenon is necessary.

Knowing God is not, however, like the return of part of the input via the output, or what is called "feedback." Neither is it a knowing that entails a binary proposition or a theory. This follows, however, from the very grammar of the expression *God*. There is such a thing as nearness to God for people. Everything else in creation is equally near God and, thus, equidistant from him. But God is to people also adjectival. All of us can become Godly, and, once more, we know this because of the very grammar of *God*. This means that we can become one in heart, disposition, and mind with God. Nearness to God is thus open to all who seek him unceasingly and without reservation. The union of a person and God forces us to another permutation on that word *know*.

Knowledge of God is somewhat akin to knowledge of oneself. What counts for knowing God is again context-determined. The person who loves deeply and long does not first have the love and then know his or her own loving and make the inference that "I am a loving person." Neither do we first have a pain and then know that we have a pain. We simply love, and in loving are clarified as persons and know what we are about and who we are. We do not know our pains, we have them. Not knowing yourself means that you suffer opaque periods when behavior is random; it means tantrums and rages; it means not knowing why you did what you did; and it means the lack of motivation and nothing accomplished. Contrariwise, it can be wanting everything at once, being unprepared for what you get, and fantasizing rather than accommodating to the way things are. Rightfully so, we can say that in these cases there is no self-knowledge. The self is not a datum about which one collects evidence. To be a self is to have wants, motives, hopes, and loves. Without these, there is nothing to know. The grammar here merges into character. But is it not this way also with God?

God is not visible—no man has seen him at any time. But God is also everywhere. He is not an object; but this does not mean that the language of faith is not a referring language. God is a spirit and a subject. (That is a grammatical remark, too.) All of us have to learn to use the language of faith referringly, for no words refer by themselves. Besides, the language of faith does not refer to objects the way mathematical numerals refer to numbers, logical notation refers to ideal entities, or science refers to physical objects. The words of faith are not just symbols, as if they were only impressive pretexts or wily simulations. To know God requires that we become "Godly." We must learn to fear him, to be observant in his presence, and then we also realize what he is. For the God of Abraham, Isaac, and Jacob, and of our Lord, Jesus Christ, is not truly known if he is not feared. This is why Kierkegaard said, and I believe truly, that Christianity requires inwardness. For fearing God means that the fears of others and of the world are cast out; but more, it becomes plainly silly to defy the Almighty God in any respect whatsoever. Thus a different attitude towards one's duties is born and also a somewhat jocular view, perhaps, of the pretensions of social and political life around us. Think, too, how one's knowledge of God grows in this instance.

More than this:

No anonymous author can more cunningly conceal himself, no practitioner of the maieutic art can more cunningly withdraw himself from the direct relationship, than God. He is in creation, and present everywhere in it, but directly He is not there; and only when the individual turns to his inner self, and hence only in the inwardness of self-activity, does he have his attention aroused, and is enabled to see God. . . . Nature, the totality of created things, is the work of God. And yet God is not there; but within the individual man there is a potentiality (man is potentially spirit) which is awakened in inwardness to become a God-relationship, and then it becomes possible to see God everywhere.[28]

The nearness of God is determined by the quality of the heart, mind, and will. He is not known in paragraphs and does not teach directly. But he does reveal the secret thoughts and hearts of all persons. The Scripture will have it that with a willing heart we can even know God's abiding presence. Then he becomes as close as the words on one's lips and the song in one's heart. The odd thing is that a true and humbling knowledge of oneself is soon involved. You must know who you are, what you can do, where

---

[28] Søren A. Kierkegaard ("Johannes Climacus"), *Concluding Unscientific Postscript*, trans. David F. Swenson and Walter Lowrie (Princeton, 1941), pp. 218–221.

you came from, and what you are about in daily life. If you know that, you soon are humbled in the awareness of pride, weak will, and, above all, sinfulness. But only in being thus humbled, in abject consciousness of ourselves, are we also likely to share God's knowledge of us. This is also what it means to become godly even in self-judgment. Surely the one who is then humbled is also the one to whom the Lord God gives his grace and his spirit (1 Peter 5:5). But this is also how one becomes a true theologian, one who actually knows God. Thus, a typical Christian prayer of confession reads: "By thy Holy Spirit increase in us true knowledge of thee and of thy will and true obedience to thy Word." That prayer limns the grammar of faith.